So You Want to Learn to Program?
Second Edition

James M. Reneau, Ph.D.
Associate Professor
Shawnee State University
Portsmouth Ohio USA

http://www.basicbook.org

James M. Reneau
P.O. Box 278
Russell, Kentucky 41169-2078 USA

For BASIC-256 Version 1.0.0.6 or later

So You Want to Learn to Program?

James M. Reneau, Ph.D. - jim@renejm.com

Table of Contents

Chapter 9: Functions and Subroutines – Reusing Code.
....125

Chapter 10: Mouse Control – Moving Things Around.
....147

Chapter 11: Keyboard Control – Using the Keyboard to Do Things..159

Chapter 12: Images, WAVs, and Sprites..................171

Index of Programs

Index of Illustrations

Acknowledgments:

A big thanks go to all the people who have worked on the BASIC-256 project, at Sourceforge. Most especially, Ian Larsen (aka: DrBlast) for creating the BASIC-256 computer language and his original vision.

I also feel the need to thank the Sumer 2010 programming kids at the Russell Middle School and Julia Moore. Also a shout to my peeps Sergey Lupin and Joel Kahn.

Dedications:

To my wife Nancy and my daughter Anna.

Credits:

Some public domain clip art from http://www.openclipart.com.

Preface

The first edition of this book was created as an introduction to programming in the BASIC language for middle to high school students who wanted to create code on their own. Over the last couple of years the text has evolved to be used in secondary and post-secondary education.

This second edition keeps most of the material in the first edition and includes the modernization of BASIC-256 to include Subroutines, Functions, and better error handling. In addition to updating the language and cleaning up the text and programs, exercises have been added to the end of each chapter to reinforce the techniques discussed and to give the readers/students an additional challenge.

This book chapters can be structured for use in a variety of ways:
1. a 9 or 18 week introduction to programming
   - chapters 1, 2, 3, 4*, 5, 6, 7, 8, and 9 for the first 9 week term
   - chapters 10, 11, 12, 13*, 14, 15, 16, 17 and 19* for the second 9 week term
2. a brief introduction to the concepts of programming
   - chapters 1, 3**, 4* , 5, 6, 7, 9, and 14
3. an introduction to data structures for non-programmers
   - chapters 1, 3**, 4* , 5, 6, 7, 9, 14, 15*, 16*, 17 and 18
4. a brief programming project for a database system course
   - chapters 1, 3**, 4* , 5, 6, 7, 9, 14, 15*, 16*, 19 and 20
5. and a brief programming project for a networking course.
   - chapters 1, 3**, 4* , 5, 6, 7, 9, 14, 15*, 16*, 19 and 21

The most important part of this book is the ability to mix and re-mix the material to fit your very specific needs.

I wish you nothing but success.
-Jim

-----

*   Denotes Optional Chapter
** Numeric Variables Section Only

Chapter 1: Meeting BASIC-256 – Say Hello.

This chapter will introduce the BASIC-256 environment using the **print** and **say** statements. You will see the difference between commands you send to the computer, strings of text, and numbers that will be used by the program. We will also explore simple mathematics to show off just how talented your computer is. Lastly you will learn what a syntax-error is and how to fix them.

The BASIC-256 Window:

The BASIC-256 window is divided into five sections: the Menu Bar, Tool Bar, Program Area, Text Output Area, and Graphics Output Area (see Illustration 1: The BASIC-256 Screen below).

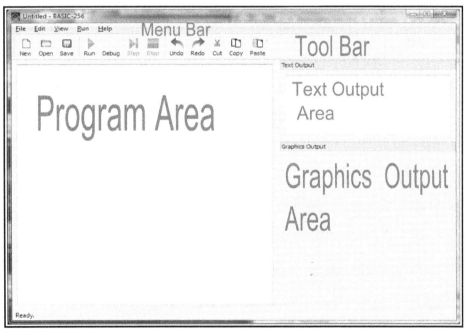

Illustration 1: The BASIC-256 Screen

Menu Bar:

The menu bar contains several different drop down menus. These menus include: "File", "Edit", "View", "Run", and "About". The "File" menu allows you to save, reload saved programs, print and exit. The "Edit" menu allows you to cut, copy and paste text and images from the program, text output, and graphics output areas. The "View" menu will allow you to show or hide various parts of the BASIC-256 window. The "Run" menu will allow you to execute and debug your programs. The "About" menu option will display a pop-up dialog with information about BASIC-256 and the version you are using.

Tool Bar:

The menu options that you will use the most are also available on the tool bar.

- New – Start a new program
- Open – Open a saved program
- Save – Save the current program to the computer's hard disk drive or your USB pen drive
- Run – Execute the currently displayed program
- Debug – Start executing program one line at a time
- Step – When debugging – go to next line
- Stop – Quit executing the current program
- Undo – Undo last change to the program.
- Redo – Redo last change that was undone.
- Cut – Move highlighted program text to the clipboard
- Copy – Place a copy of the highlighted program text on the clipboard

- Paste – Insert text from the clipboard into program at current insertion point

Program Area:

Programs are made up of instructions to tell the computer exactly what to do and how to do it. You will type your programs, modify and fix your code, and load saved programs into this area of the screen.

Text Output Area:

This area will display the output of your programs. This may include words and numbers. If the program needs to ask you a question, the question (and what you type) will be displayed here.

Graphics Output Area:

BASIC-256 is a graphical language (as you will see). Pictures, shapes, and graphics you will create will be displayed here.

Your first program – The *say* statement:

Let's actually write a computer program. Let us see if BASIC-256 will say hello to us. In the Program Area type the following one-line program (you will see the line number in BASIC256 but you should not type it):

```
1      say "hello"
```
Program 1: Say Hello

Once you have this program typed in, use the mouse, and click on
"Run" in the tool bar.

Did BASIC-256 say hello to you through the computer's speakers?

```
say expression
```

The **say** statement is used to make BASIC-256 read an expression aloud, to the computer's speakers.

"letters, numbers 9988, and symbols &%"
'another string with a "quote" inside.'

BASIC-256 treats letters, numbers, and punctuation that are inside a set of quotation marks as a block. This block is called a *string*.

A string may begin with either a single quote mark (') or a double quote mark (") and ends the same as it began. A string surrounded with single quotes may contain double quotes and a string surrounded by double quotes may contain single quotes.

▷ "Run" on the tool bar - or - "<u>R</u>un" then "<u>R</u>un" on the menu

You must tell BASIC-256 when you want it to start executing a program. It doesn't automatically know when you are done typing your programming code in. You do this by clicking on the

▷ "Run" icon on the tool bar or by clicking on "<u>R</u>un" from the menu bar then selecting "<u>R</u>un" from the drop down menu.

To clear out the program you are working on and completely start a new program we use the [ ] "New" button on the tool bar. The new button will display the following dialog box:

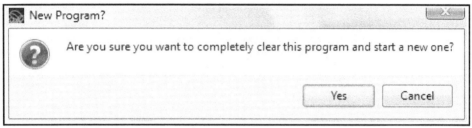

Illustration 2: BASIC-256 - New Dialog

If you are fine with clearing your program from the screen then click on the | Yes | "Yes" button.   If you accidentally hit "New" and do not want to start a new program then click on the | Cancel | "Cancel" button.

New Concept

"New" on the tool bar - or - "File" then "New" on the menu

The "New" command tells BASIC-256 that you want to clear the current statements from the program area and start a totally new program. If you have not saved your program to the computer (Chapter 2) then you will lose all changes you have made to the program.

You can also have the **say** statement speak out numbers. Try the following program:

```
1       say 123456789
```

Program 2: Say a Number

Once you have this program typed in, use the mouse, and click on
"Run" in the tool bar.

Did BASIC-256 say what you were expecting?

	numbers
	BASIC-256 allows you to enter numbers in decimal format. Do not use commas when you are entering large numbers. If you need a number less than zero just place the negative sign before the number.
New Concept	Examples include: 1.56, 23456, -6.45 and .5

BASIC-256 is really good with numbers – Simple Arithmetic:

The brain of the computer (called the Central Processing Unit or CPU for short) works exclusively with numbers. Everything it does from graphics, sound, and all the rest is done by manipulating numbers.

The four basic operations of addition, subtraction, multiplication, and division are carried out using the operators show in Table 1.

Operator	Operation
+	Addition expression1 + expression2
-	Subtraction expression1 - expression2
*	Multiplication expression1 * expression2
/	Division expression1 / expression2

Table 1: Basic Mathematical Operators

Try this program and listen to the talking super calculator.

```
1      say 12 * (2 + 10)
```
Program 3: Say the Answer

The computer should have said "144" to you.

```
1      say 5 / 2
```
Program 4: Say another Answer

Did the computer say "2.5"?

+
−
*
/
()

The four basic mathematical operations: addition (+), subtraction (-), division (/), and multiplication(*) work with numbers to perform calculations. A numeric value is required on both sides of these operators. You may also use parenthesis to group operations together.

Examples include: 1 + 1, 5 * 7, 3.14 * 6 + 2, (1 + 2) * 3 and 5 - 5

Another use for + (Concatenation):

The + operator also will add strings together. This operation is called concatenation, or "cat" for short. When we concatenate we are joining the strings together, like train cars, to make a longer string.

Let's try it out:

```
1      say "Hello " + "Bob."
```
Program 5: Say Hello to Bob

The computer should have said hello to Bob.

Try another.

```
1      say 1 + " more time"
```
Program 6: Say it One More Time

The + in the last example was used as the concatenate operator because the second term was a string and the computer does not know how to perform mathematics with a string (so it 'cats').

+ (concatenate)

Another use for the the plus sign (+) is to tell the computer to concatenate (join) strings together. If one or both operands are a string, concatenation will be performed; if both operands are numeric, then addition is performed.

New Concept

The text output area - The print statement:

Programs that use the Text to Speech (TTS) **say** statement can be very useful and fun but is is also often necessary to write information (strings and numbers) to the screen so that the output can be read. The **print** statement does just that. In the Program Area type the following two-line program:

```
1     print "hello"
2     print "there"
```

Program 7: Print Hello There

Once you have this program typed in, use the mouse, and click on ▶ "Run" in the tool bar. The text output area should now show "hello" on the first line and "there" on the second line.

```
print expression
print expression;
```

The **print** statement is used to display text and numbers on the text output area of the BASIC-256 window. **Print** normally goes down to the next line but you may print several things on the same line by using a ; (semicolon) at the end of the *expression*.

The **print** statement, by default, advances the text area so that the next **print** is on the next line. If you place a ; (semicolon) on the end of the *expression* being printed, it will suppress the line advance so that the next **print** will be on the same line.

```
1    cls
2    print "Hello ";
3    print "there, ";
4    print "my friend."
```

Program 8: Many Prints One Line

```
cls
```

The *cls* statement clears all of the old displayed information from the text output area.

What is a "Syntax error":

Programmers are human and occasionally make mistakes. "Syntax errors" are one of the types of errors that we may encounter. A "Syntax error" is generated by BASIC-256 when it does not understand the program you have typed in. Usually syntax errors are caused by misspellings, missing commas, incorrect spaces, unclosed quotations, or unbalanced parenthesis. BASIC-256 will tell you what line your error is on and will even attempt to tell you where on the line the error is.

Exercises:

Word Search

```
z a h d g p b a n n q m c
j g j r o i q l o c q o x
r u n t u u n i l c n s z
v w s y o b s s k c y l l
e n a t i s s p a n p a x
r s e p e q r t t f r p t
r b k r y o e a r m m r a
o r p i g n x d o i f n i
r x n r a y t i h l n a f
e g a t m d w n v e d g i
t m i a c v c e i j f d n
b o t c c a u s o r c i s
n a m z i z i g n c p r u
```

cls, concatenation, error, expression, print, program, quote, run, say, stop, string, syntax

Problems

1.1. Write a one line program to say the tongue twister 'Peter Piper picked a peck of pickled peppers."

1.2. Add a second line to Problem 1.1 to also display that sentence on the screen.

1.3. Use the computer as a talking calculator to solve the following problem and to say the answer: Bob has 5 pieces of candy and Jim has 9. If they were to share the candy evenly between them, how many would they each have (average).

1.4. Use the computer as a talking calculator to solve the following problem and to say the answer: You want 5 model cars that each cost $1.25 and one model boat that costs $3.50. How much

| | money to you need to make these purchases. |
| | 1.5. Write a one line program to say "one plus two equals three" without using the word three or the number 3. |

Chapter 2: Drawing Basic Shapes.

In this chapter we will be getting graphical. You will learn how to draw rectangles, circles, lines and points of various colors. These programs will get more and more complex, so you will also learn how to save your programs to long term storage and how to load them back in so you can run them again or change them.

Drawing Rectangles and Circles:

Let's start the graphics off by writing a graphical program for our favorite sports team, the "Grey Spots". Their colors are blue and grey.

```
1  # c2_greyspots.kbs
2  # a program for our team - the grey spots
3
4  clg
5  color blue
6  rect 0,0,300,300
7  color grey
8  circle 149,149,100
9  say "Grey Spots, Grey Spots, Grey spots rule!"
```

Program 9: Grey Spots

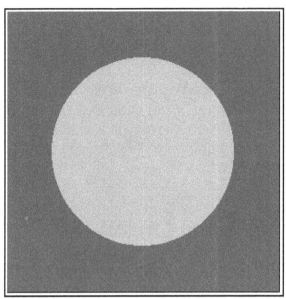

Sample Output 9: Grey Spots

Let's go line by line through the program above. The first line is called a remark or comment statement. A remark is a place for the programmer to place comments in their computer code that are ignored by the system. Remarks are a good place to describe what complex blocks of code is doing, the program's name, why we wrote a program, or who the programmer was.

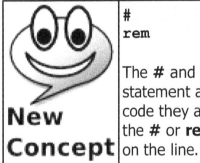

```
#
rem
```

The **#** and **rem** statements are called remarks. A remark statement allows the programmer to put comments about the code they are working on into the program. The computer sees the **#** or **rem** statement and will ignore all of the rest of the text on the line.

On line two you see the **clg** statement. It is much like the **cls** statement from Chapter 1, except that the **clg** statement will clear the graphic output area of the screen.

New Concept

```
clg
```

The **clg** statement erases the graphics output area so that we have a clean place to do our drawings.

Lines four and six contain the simple form of the **color** statement. It tells BASIC-256 what color to use for the next drawing action. You may define colors either by using one of the eighteen standard color names or you may create one of over 16 million different colors by mixing the primary colors of light (red, green, and blue) together.

When you are using the numeric method to define your custom color be sure to limit the values from 0 to 255. Zero (0) represents no light of that component color and 255 means to shine the maximum. Bright white is represented by 255, 255, 255 (all colors of light) where black is represented by 0, 0, 0 (no colors at all). This numeric representation is known as the RGB triplet. Illustration 5 shows the named colors and their RGB values.

New Concept

```
color color_name
color rgb( red, green, blue )
```

color can also be spelled **colour**.

The **color** statement allows you to set the color that will be drawn next. You may follow the **color** statement with a color name (black, white, red, darkred, green, darkgreen, blue, darkblue, cyan, darkcyan, purple, darkpurple, yellow, darkyellow, orange, darkorange, grey/gray, darkgrey/darkgray). You may also specify over 16 million different colors using the RGB() function by specifying how much red, blue, and green should be used.

Color Name and RGB Values		Color Name and RGB Values	
black (0,0,0)	■	white (255,255,255)	
red (255,0,0)	■	darkred (128,0,0)	■
Green (0,255,0)		darkgreen (0,128,0)	■
blue (0,0,255)	■	darkblue (0,0,128)	■
cyan (0,255,255)		darkcyan (0,128,128)	■
purple (255,0,255)	■	darkpurple (128,0,128)	■
yellow (255,255,0)		darkyellow (128,128,0)	■
orange (255,102,0)	■	darkorange (170,51,0)	■
grey/gray (164,164,164)	■	darkgrey/darkgray (128,128,128)	■

Illustration 3: Color Names

The graphics display area, by default is 300 pixels wide (x) by 300 pixels high (y). A pixel is the smallest dot that can be displayed on your computer monitor. The top left corner is the origin (0,0) and the bottom right is (299,299). Each pixel can be represented by two numbers, the first (x) is how far over it is and the second (y) represents how far down. This way of marking points is known as the Cartesian Coordinate System to mathematicians.

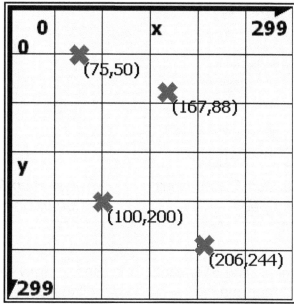

Illustration 4: The Cartesian Coordinate System of the Graphics Output Area

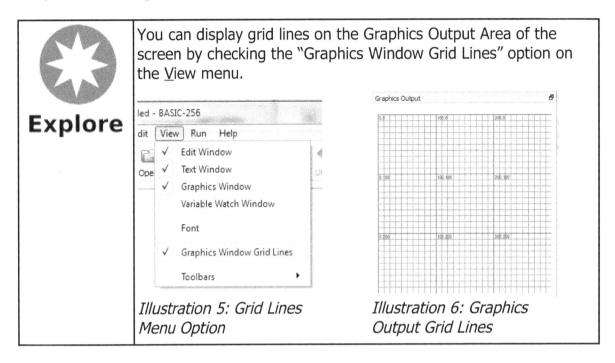

You can display grid lines on the Graphics Output Area of the screen by checking the "Graphics Window Grid Lines" option on the <u>V</u>iew menu.

Illustration 5: Grid Lines Menu Option

Illustration 6: Graphics Output Grid Lines

The next statement (line 5) is **rect**. It is used to draw rectangles on the screen. It takes four numbers separated by commas; (1) how far over the left side of the rectangle is from the left edge of the graphics area, (2) how far down the top edge is, (3) how wide and (4) how tall. All four numbers are expressed in pixels (the size of the smallest dot that can be displayed).

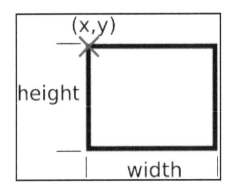

Illustration 7: Rectangle

You can see the the rectangle in the program starts in the top left corner and fills the graphics output area.

 **New Concept**	`rect x, y, width, height` The **rect** statement uses the current drawing color and places a rectangle on the graphics output window. The top left corner of the rectangle is specified by the first two numbers and the width and height is specified by the other two arguments.

Line 7 of Program 9 introduces the **circle** statement to draw a circle. It takes three numeric arguments, the first two represent the Cartesian coordinates for the center of the circle and the third the radius in pixels.

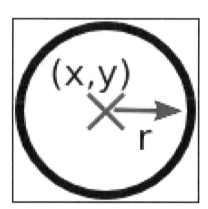

Illustration 8: Circle

```
circle x, y, radius
```

The **circle** statement uses the current drawing color and draws a filled circle with its center at (x, y) with the specified radius.

New Concept

Here are a couple of sample programs that use the new statements **clg**, **color**, **rect** and **circle**. Type the programs in and modify them. Make them a frowning face, alien face, or look like somebody you know.

```
1    # c2_rectanglesmile.kbs
2    # draw a smiling face with rectangles
3
4    # clear the screen
5    clg
6
7    # draw the face
8    color yellow
9    rect 0,0,299,299
10
11   # draw the mouth
12   color black
13   rect 100,200,100,25
14
15   # put on the eyes
16   color black
17   rect 75,75,50,50
18   rect 175,75,50,50
19
20   say "Hello."
```

Program 10: Face with Rectangles

Sample Output 10: Face with Rectangles

```
1    # c2_circlesmile.kbs
2    # smiling face made with circles
3
4    # clear the screen
5    clg
6    color white
7    rect 0,0,300,300
8
9    # draw the face
10   color yellow
11   circle 150,150,150
12
13   # draw the mouth
14   color black
15   circle 150,200,70
16   color yellow
```

```
17     circle 150,150,70
18
19     # put on the eyes
20     color black
21     circle 100,100,30
22     circle 200,100,30
```

Program 11: Smiling Face with Circles

Sample Output 11: Smiling Face with Circles

Saving Your Program and Loading it Back:

Now that the programs are getting more complex, you may want to save them so that you can load them back in the future.

You may store a program by using the Save button  on the tool bar or Save option on the File menu. A dialog will display asking you for a file name, if it is a new program, or will save the changes you have made (replacing the old file).

If you do not want to replace the old version of the program and you want to store it using a new name you may use the Save <u>A</u>s option on the <u>F</u>ile menu to save a copy with a different name.

To load a previously saved program you would use the Open button on the tool bar or the <u>O</u>pen option on the <u>F</u>ile menu.

Drawing with Lines:

The next drawing statement is **line**. It will draw a line one pixel wide, of the current color, from one point to another point. Program 12 shows an example of how to use the **line** statement.

```
1    # c2_triangle.kbs
2    # draw a triangle
3
4    clg
5    color black
6
7    line 150, 100, 100, 200
8    line 100, 200, 200, 200
9    line 200, 200, 150, 100
```

Program 12: Draw a Triangle

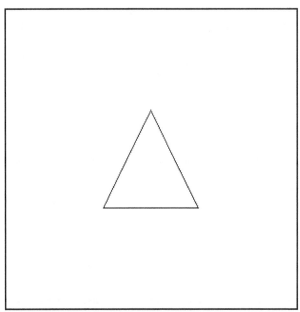

Sample Output 12: Draw a Triangle

 **New Concept**

```
line start_x, start_y, finish_x, finish_y
```

Draw a line one pixel wide from the starting point to the ending point, using the current color.

The next program is a sample of what you can do with complex lines. It draws a cube on the screen.

```
1    # c2_cube.kbs
2    # use lines to draw a 3d cube
3
4    clg
```

```
5        color black
6
7        # draw back square
8        line 150, 150, 150, 250
9        line 150, 250, 250, 250
10       line 250, 250, 250, 150
11       line 250, 150, 150, 150
12
13       # draw front square
14       line 100, 100, 100, 200
15       line 100, 200, 200, 200
16       line 200, 200, 200, 100
17       line 200, 100, 100, 100
18
19       # connect the corners
20       line 100, 100, 150, 150
21       line 100, 200, 150, 250
22       line 200, 200, 250, 250
23       line 200, 100, 250, 150
```

Program 13: Draw a Cube

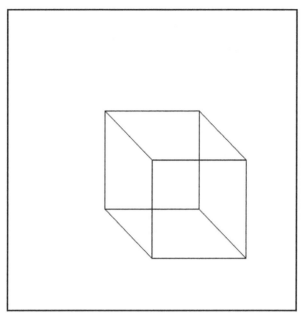

Sample Output 13: Draw a Cube

Setting Line Width and Drawing Shape Borders:

By default the width of a line drawn in BASIC256 is one pixel (dot) wide. The **penwidth** statement can be used to change the way lines (and borders around shapes) are drawn.

The following program will illustrate the **penwidth** statement, a more complex use of the **color** statement and an example of the special color **clear**.

```
1    # c2_shapeoutline.kbs
2    # draw a shape with an outline
3
4    clg
5
6    penwidth 7
7    color blue, rgb(255,128,128)
8    circle 100,50,44
```

```
9
10      color black
11      penwidth 5
12      line 50,50,250,250
13
14      color red
15      penwidth 10
16      line 175,100,100,175
17
18      color green, clear
19      penwidth 10
20      rect 150,175,75,75
```

Program 14: Penwidth and Shape Outline

Sample Output 14: Penwidth and Shape Outline

```
penwidth n
```

Changes the width of the drawing pen. The pen represents the width of a line being drawn and also the width of the outline of a shape.

New Concept

```
color pen_color, fill_color
```

Earlier in this chapter we saw the color statement with a single color. When only a single color is specified then both the pen and the fill color are set to the same value. You may define the pen and fill colors to be different colors by using the color statement with two colors.

New Concept

```
clear
```

The word clear may be used in the color statement to tell BASIC256 to only draw the border of a shape. This is accomplished by setting the fill color to clear.

New Concept

Setting Individual Points on the Screen:

The last graphics statement covered in this chapter is **plot**. The **plot** statement sets a single pixel (dot) on the screen. For most of us these are so

small, they are hard to see. Later we will write programs that will draw
groups of pixels to make very detailed images.

```
1      # c2_plot.kbs
2      # use plot to draw points
3
4      clg
5
6      color red
7      plot 99,100
8      plot 100,99
9      plot 100,100
10     plot 100,101
11     plot 101,100
12
13     color darkgreen
14     plot 200,200
```

Program 15: Use Plot to Draw Points

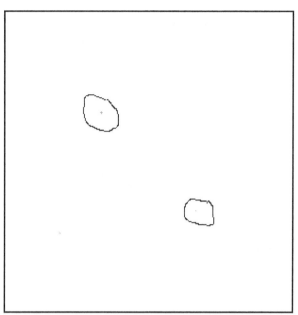

Sample Output 15: Use Plot to Draw Points (circled for emphasis)

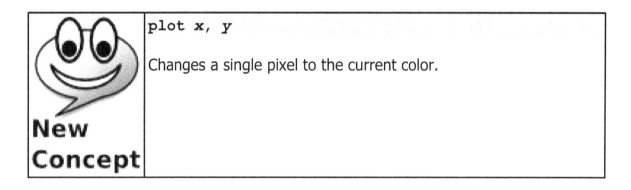

```
plot x, y
```

Changes a single pixel to the current color.

Big Program

At the end of each chapter there will be one or more big programs for you to look at, type in, and experiment with. These programs will contain only topics that we have covered so far in the book.

This "Big Program" takes the idea of a face and makes it talk. Before the program will say each word the lower half of the face is redrawn with a different mouth shape. This creates a rough animation and makes the face more fun.

```
1    # c2_talkingface.kbs
2    # draw face background with eyes
3
4    color yellow
5    rect 0,0,300,300
6    color black
7    rect 75,75,50,50
8    rect 175,75,50,50
9
10   # erase old mouth
11   color yellow
12   rect 0,150,300,150
13   # draw new mouth
14   color black
15   rect 125,175,50,100
16   # say word
17   say "i"
18
19   color yellow
20   rect 0,150,300,150
21   color black
22   rect 100,200,100,50
23   say "am"
24
25   color yellow
26   rect 0,150,300,150
27   color black
28   rect 125,175,50,100
```

```
29      say "glad"
30
31      color yellow
32      rect 0,150,300,150
33      color black
34      rect 125,200,50,50
35      say "you"
36
37      color yellow
38      rect 0,150,300,150
39      color black
40      rect 100,200,100,50
41      say "are"
42
43      color yellow
44      rect 0,150,300,150
45      color black
46      rect 125,200,50,50
47      say "my"
48
49      # draw whole new face with round smile.
50      color yellow
51      rect 0,0,300,300
52      color black
53      circle 150,175,100
54      color yellow
55      circle 150,150,100
56      color black
57      rect 75,75,50,50
58      rect 175,75,50,50
59      say "friend"
```

Program 16: Big Program - Talking Face

Sample Output 16: Big Program - Talking Face

Exercises:

Word Search

```
r  e  t  a  n  i  d  r  o  o  c
e  e  a  r  a  e  l  c  r  u  m
m  e  l  c  r  i  c  e  s  s  r
a  c  k  v  c  e  c  c  u  y  o
r  y  j  l  n  t  i  i  t  p  l
k  a  g  t  a  h  d  h  w  l  o
q  n  e  n  p  a  g  i  q  o  c
y  r  g  a  r  i  d  p  j  t  e
c  l  r  e  e  t  s  a  v  e  h
e  g  p  h  h  u  e  n  i  l  d
j  r  x  p  e  n  w  i  d  t  h
```

center, circle, clear, clg, color, coordinate, cyan, graphics, height, line, penwidth, plot, radius, rectangle, remark, save, width

Problems

2.1. Type in the code for Program 11: Smiling Face with Circles (on page 24) and modify it to display Mr. Yuck. You may need to use the **penwidth** statement to make the lines you draw thicker.

2.2. Write a program to draw a square and then say "square". Clear the graphics screen, draw a circle, and say "circle". Then clear the graphics screen draw several lines (in any pattern you would like) and say "lines".

2.3. Use colors, lines, and circles to draw an archery target with an arrow in the center. Once the arrow is drawn make the computer say "Bullseye!".

2.4. Write a program that draws each of the quarters of the moon (new moon, first quarter, full moon, and third quarter) and speaks the name for the quarter. Hint: Draw the moon as a circle and then draw a rectangle over the part you do not want.

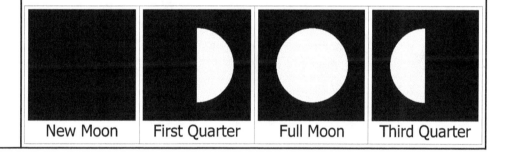

| New Moon | First Quarter | Full Moon | Third Quarter |

Chapter 3: Sound and Music.

Now that we have color and graphics, let's add sound and make some music. Basic concepts of the physics of sound, numeric variables, and musical notation will be introduced. You will be able to translate a tune into frequencies and durations to have the computer synthesize a voice.

Sound Basics – Things you need to know about sound:

Sound is created by vibrating air striking your ear-drum. These vibrations are known as sound waves. When the air is vibrating quickly you will hear a high note and when the air is vibrating slowly you will hear a low note. The rate of the vibration is called frequency.

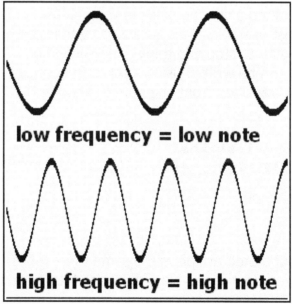

Illustration 9: Sound Waves

Frequency is measured in a unit called hertz (Hz). It represents how many cycles (ups and downs) a wave vibrates through in a second. A normal person can hear very low sounds at 20 Hz and very high sounds at 20,000 Hz. BASIC-256 can produce tones in the range of 50Hz to 7000Hz.

Another property of a sound is its length. Computers are very fast and can measure times accurately to a millisecond (ms). A millisecond (ms) is 1/1000 (one thousandths) of a second.

Let's make some sounds.

```
1      # c3_sounds.kbs
2      sound 233, 1000
3      sound 466, 500
4      sound 233, 1000
```

Program 17: Play Three Individual Notes

You may have heard a clicking noise in your speakers between the notes played in the last example. This is caused by the computer creating the sound and needing to stop and think a millisecond or so. The *sound* statement also can be written using a list of frequencies and durations to smooth out the transition from one note to another.

```
1      # c3_soundslist.kbs
2      sound {233, 1000, 466, 500, 233, 1000}
```

Program 18: List of Sounds

This second sound program plays the same three tones for the same duration but the computer creates and plays all of the sounds at once, making them smoother.

New Concept

```
sound frequency, duration
sound {frequency1, duration1, frequency2,
    duration2 ...}
sound numeric_array
```

The basic *sound* statement takes two arguments; (1) the frequency of the sound in Hz (cycles per second) and (2) the length of the tone in milliseconds (ms). The second form of the sound statement uses curly braces and can specify several tones and durations in a list. The third form of the sound statement uses an array containing frequencies and durations. Arrays are covered in Chapter 11.

How do we get BASIC-256 to play a tune? The first thing we need to do is to convert the notes on a music staff to frequencies. Illustration 9 shows two octaves of music notes, their names, and the approximate frequency the note makes. In music you will also find a special mark called the rest. The rest means not to play anything for a certain duration. If you are using a list of sounds you can insert a rest by specifying a frequency of zero (0) and the needed duration for the silence.

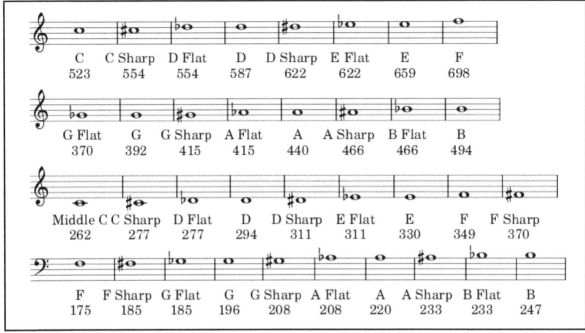

Illustration 10: Musical Notes

Take a little piece of music and then look up the frequency values for each of the notes. Why don't we have the computer play "Charge!". The music is in Illustration 11. You might notice that the high G in the music is not on the musical notes; if a note is not on the chart you can double (to make higher) or half (to make lower) the same note from one octave away.

Illustration 11: Charge!

Now that we have the frequencies we need the duration for each of the notes. Table 2 shows most of the common note and rest symbols, how long they are when compared to each other, and a few typical durations.

Duration in milliseconds (ms) can be calculated if you know the speed if the music in beats per minute (BPM) using Formula 1.

$$Note\ Duration = 1000 * 60 / Beats\ Per\ Minute * Relative\ Length$$

Formula 1: Calculating Note Duration

Note Name	Symbols for Note - Rest	Length	At 100 BPM	At 120 BPM	At 140 BPM
Dotted Whole		6.000	3600 ms	3000 ms	2571 ms
Whole		4.000	2400 ms	2000 ms	1714 ms
Dotted Half		3.000	1800 ms	1500 ms	1285 ms
Half		2.000	1200 ms	1000 ms	857 ms
Dotted Quarter		1.500	900 ms	750 ms	642 ms
Quarter		1.000	600 ms	500 ms	428 ms
Dotted Eighth		0.750	450 ms	375 ms	321 ms
Eighth		0.500	300 ms	250 ms	214 ms
Dotted Sixteenth		0.375	225 ms	187 ms	160 ms
Sixteenth		0.250	150 ms	125 ms	107 ms

Table 2: Musical Notes and Typical Durations

Now with the formula and table to calculate note durations, we can write the program to play "Charge!".

```
1      # c3_charge.kbs
2      # play charge
3
4      sound {392, 375, 523, 375, 659, 375, 784, 250, 659,
       250, 784, 250}
5      say "Charge!"
```

Program 19: Charge!

Numeric Variables:

Computers are really good at remembering things, where we humans sometimes have trouble. The BASIC language allows us to give names to places in the computer's memory and then store information in them. These places are called variables.

There are four types of variables: numeric variables, string variables, numeric array variables, and string array variables. You will learn how to use numeric variables in this chapter and the others in later chapters.

Numeric variable

A numeric variable allows you to assign a name to a block of storage in the computer's short-term memory. You may store and retrieve numeric (whole or decimal) values from these variables in your program.

A numeric variable name must begin with a letter; may contain letters and numbers; and are case sensitive. You may not use words reserved by the BASIC-256 language when naming your variables (see Appendix I).

Examples of valid variable names include: a, b6, reader, x, and zoo.

Variable names are case sensitive. This means that an upper case variable and a lowercase variable with the same letters do not represent the same location in the computer's memory.

Program 20 is an example of a program using numeric variables.

```
1    # c3_numericvariables.kbs
2    # use numeric variables
3
4    let numerator = 30
5    let denominator = 5
6    let result = numerator / denominator
7    print result
```

Program 20: Simple Numeric Variables

The program above uses three variables. On line two it stores the value 30 into the location named "numerator". Line three stores the value 5 in the variable "denominator". Line four takes the value from "numerator" divides it by the value in the "denominator" variable and stores the value in the variable named "result".

New Concept

```
let variable = expression
variable = expression
```

The **let** statement will calculate an expression (if necessary) and saves the value into a variable. We call this process assignment or assigning a variable.

The variable on the left hand side of the equal sign will take on the value of the variable, number, function, or mathematical expression on the right hand side of the equal sign.

The actual **let** statement is optional. You can just assign a variable using the equal sign.

```
1     let a = 7
2     let b = a / 2 + .7
3     print a + b
```

Program 21: Simple Variable Assignment

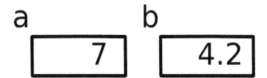

Sample Output 21: Simple Variable Assignment

The statements Program 21 will create two storage locations in memory and store the value or the result of the calculation in them. Line three of the program will add the values together and print the value 11.2. You may use a numeric variable anywhere you need a number and the value in the variable will be pulled from memory.

Variables are called variables because they can be changed as a program runs. Look at the example in Program 22 (below) In line 1 the variable z is assigned the value 99. In line 2 the expression z -1 is calculated and the result is stored back in z. In the last line the value of z is printed, Can you guess what that will be?

```
1    z = 99
2    z = z - 1
3    print z
```

Program 22: Variable Re-assignment

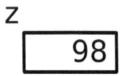

Sample Output 22: Variable Re-assignment

Variables and their associated values persist, once they are created, for the remainder of the time a program is running. Once a program stops (either completes or errors) the variables values are emptied and the memory is returned to the computer's operating system to be assigned for future tasks.

Now that we have learned a bit more about variables we could re-write the "Charge!" program using variables and the formula to calculate note durations (Formula 1).

```
1    # c3_charge2.kbs
2    # play charge - use variables
3
4    beats = 120
5    dottedeighth = 1000 * 60 / beats * .75
6    eighth = 1000 * 60 / beats * .5
7
8    sound {392, dottedeighth, 523, dottedeighth, 659,
     dottedeighth, 784, eighth, 659, eighth, 784, eighth}
9    say "Charge!"
```

Program 23: Charge! with Variables

Variable Assignment Shortcuts:

Another thing you will learn about computer programming is that there are often more than one way do do a task. BASIC-256 and most computer programming languages allow for a shortcut form of addition and subtraction when working with a variable. In the programs of future chapters you will see these shortcuts.

Shortcut Assignment	Longhand Assignment
variable+=expression a+=9	variable = variable + expression a = a + 9
variable -= expression b -= a+2	variable = variable - expression b = b - (a + 2)
variable++ foo++	variable = variable + 1 foo = foo + 1
Variable-- bar--	Variable = variable − 1 bar = bar - 1

Table 3: Shortcut Variable Assignments

Big Program

For this chapter's big program let's take a piece of music by J.S. Bach and write a program to play it.

The musical score is a part of J.S. Bach's Little Fuge in G.

Illustration 12: First Four Measures of J.S. Bach's Little Fuge in G

```
1      # c3_littlefuge.kbs
2      # Music by J.S.Bach - XVIII Fuge in G moll.
3
```

```
4      tempo = 100 # beats per minute
5      milimin = 1000 * 60 # miliseconds in a minute
6      q = milimin / tempo # quarter note is a beat
7      h = q * 2 # half note (2 quarters)
8      e = q / 2 # eight note (1/2 quarter)
9      s = q / 4 # sixteenth note (1/4 quarter)
10     de = e + s # dotted eight - eight + 16th
11     dq = q + e # doted quarter - quarter + eight
12
13     sound{392, q, 587, q, 466, dq, 440, e, 392, e, 466,
       e, 440, e, 392, e, 370, e, 440, e, 294, q, 392, e,
       294, e, 440, e, 294, e, 466, e, 440, s, 392, s, 440,
       e, 294, e, 392, e, 294, s, 392, s, 440, e, 294, s,
       440, s, 466, e, 440, s, 392, s, 440, s, 294, s}
```

Program 24: Big Program - Little Fuge in G

Exercises:

Word Search

```
d j r a h e r t z q y t x
n a v a r i a b l e l z s
o s h a l f n g k j u e x
c s s h o r t c u t c g j
e i e h t h g i e a h i n
s g t u r l s l r t b k x
i n a t y f i b n d e d t
l m r s a i x e n e x l u
l e b y c n e u q e r f i
i n i b q t o e v a t c o
m t v z x s j w h o l e b
m u s i c r e t r a u q a
i j s q s e y t e t o n t
```

assignment, braces, eighth, frequency, half, hertz, millisecond, music, note, octave, quarter, shortcut, sixteenth, sound, variable, vibrate, whole

Problems

3.1. Write a program using a single sound statement to play "Shave and a Hair Cut". Remember you must include the quarter rests in the second measure in your sound with a frequency of zero and the duration of a quarter note.

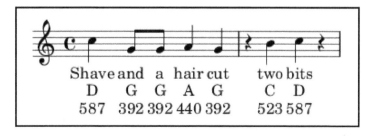

3.2. Type the sound statement below and insert the variable assignments before it to play "Row Row Row your Boat". The variables c, d, e, f, g, and cc should contain the frequency of the notes of the tune. The variable n4 should contain the length in milliseconds of a quarter note; n2 twice n4, and n8 one half of n4.

```
sound {c,n4+n8, c,n4+n8, c,n4, d,n8, e,n4+n8,
e,n4, d,n8, e,n4, f,n8, g,n2+n4, cc,n8, cc,n8,
cc,n8, g,n8, g,n8, g,n8, e,n8, e,n8, e,n8, c,n8,
c,n8, c,n8, g,n4, f,n8, d,n4, e,n8, c,n2+n4}
```

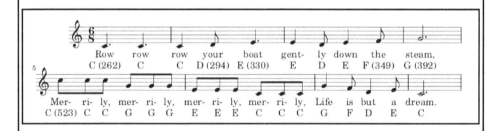

3.3. Create a program with two variables 'a' and 'b' that you will assign to two numbers. Print the sum of a and b, the difference of a and b, the difference of b and a, the product of a and b, the quotient of a divided by b, and the quotient of b divided by a. Run the program with several different values of a and b. What happens when a or b are set to the value of zero?

Chapter 4: Thinking Like a Programmer

One of the hardest things to learn is how to think like a programmer. A programmer is not created by simple books or classes but grows from within an individual. To become a "good" programmer takes passion for technology, self learning, basic intelligence, and a drive to create and explore.

You are like the great explorers Christopher Columbus, Neil Armstrong, and Yuri Gagarin (the first human in space). You have an unlimited universe to explore and to create within the computer. The only restrictions on where you can go will be your creativity and willingness to learn.

A program to develop a game or interesting application can often exceed several thousand lines of computer code. This can very quickly become overwhelming, even to the most experienced programmer. Often we programmers will approach a complex problem using a three step process, like:

1.   Think about the problem.
2.   Break the problem up into pieces and write them down formally.
3.   Convert the pieces into the computer language you are using.

Pseudocode:

Pseudocode is a fancy word for writing out, step by step, what your program needs to be doing. The word pseudocode comes from the Greek prefix "pseudo-" meaning fake and "code" for the actual computer programming statements. It is not created for the computer to use directly but it is made to help you understand the complexity of a problem and to break it down into meaningful pieces.

There is no single best way to write pseudocode. Dozens of standards exist and each one of them is very suited for a particular type of problem. In this introduction we will use simple English statements to understand our problems.

How would you go about writing a simple program to draw a school bus (like in Illustration 13)?

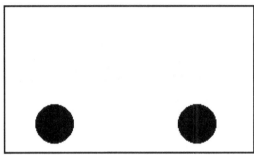

Illustration 13: School Bus

Let's break this problem into two steps:

- draw the wheels
- draw the body

Now let's break the initial steps into smaller pieces and write our pseudocode:

Set color to black. Draw both wheels. Set color to yellow. Draw body of bus. Draw the front of bus.

Table 4: School Bus - Pseudocode

Now that we have our program worked out, all we need to do is write it:

Set color to black. Draw both wheels.	color black circle 50,120,20 circle 200,120,20
Set color to yellow. Draw body of bus. Draw the front of bus.	color yellow rect 50,0,200,100 rect 0,50,50,50

Table 5: School Bus - Pseudocode with BASIC-256 Statements

The completed school bus program (Program 25) is listed below. Look at the finished program and you will see comment statements used in the program to help the programmer remember the steps used during the initial problem solving.

```
1    # c4_schoolbus.kbs
2    # draw a school bus
3
4    clg
5
6    # draw wheels
7    color black
8    circle 50,120,20
9    circle 200,120,20
10
11   # draw bus body
12   color yellow
13   rect 50,0,200,100
14   rect 0,50,50,50
```

Program 25: School Bus

In the school bus example we have just seen there were many different ways to break up the problem. You could have drawn the bus first and the wheels last, you could have drawn the front before the back,... We could list dozens of different ways this simple problem could have been tackled.

One very important thing to remember, THERE IS NO WRONG WAY to approach a problem. Some ways are better than others (fewer instructions, easier to read, …), but the important thing is that you solved the problem.

Flowcharting:

Another technique that programmers use to understand a problem is called flowcharting. Following the old adage of "a picture is worth a thousand words", programmers will sometimes draw a diagram representing the logic of a program. Flowcharting is one of the oldest and commonly used methods of drawing this structure.

This brief introduction to flowcharts will only cover a small part of what that can be done with them, but with a few simple symbols and connectors you will be able to model very complex processes. This technique will serve you well not only in programming but in solving many problems you will come across. Here are a few of the basic symbols:

Symbol	Name and Description
(flow arrow symbol)	Flow – An arrow represents moving from one symbol or step in the process to another. You must follow the direction of the arrowhead.
Terminator	Terminator – This symbol tells us where to start and finish the flowchart. Each flowchart should have two of these: a start and a finish.
Process	Process – This symbol represents activities or actions that the program will need to take. There should be only one arrow leaving a process.
Input and Output	Input and Output (I/O) – This symbol represents data or items being read by the system or being written out of the system. An example would be saving or loading files.
Decision	Decision – The decision diamond asks a simple yes/no or true/false question. There should be two arrows that leave a decision. Depending on the result of the question we will follow one path out of the diamond.

Table 6: Essential Flowcharting Symbols

The best way to learn to flowchart is to look at some examples and to try your own hand it it.

Flowcharting Example One:

You just rolled out of bed and your mom has given you two choices for breakfast. You can have your favorite cold cereal or a scrambled egg. If you do not choose one of those options you can go to school hungry.

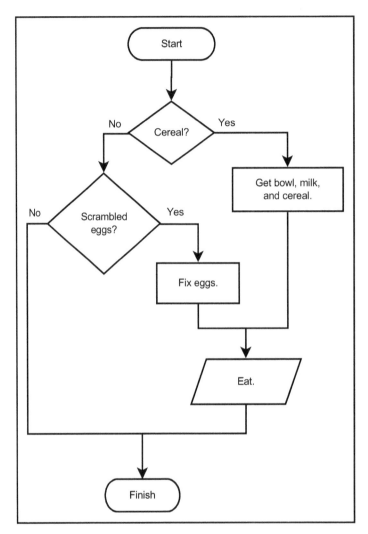

Illustration 14: Breakfast - Flowchart

Take a look at Illustration 14 (above) and follow all of the arrows. Do you see how that picture represents the scenario?

Flowcharting Example Two:

Another food example. You are thirsty and want a soda from the machine.
Take a look at Illustration 15 (below).

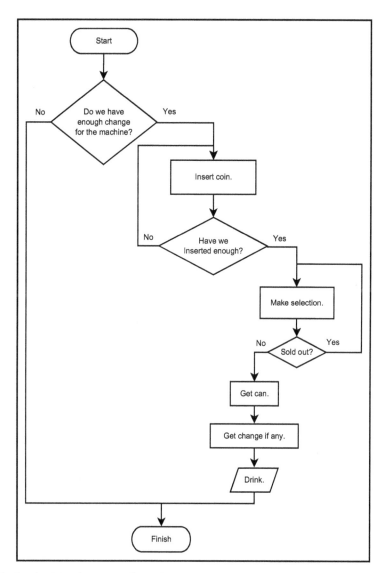

Illustration 15: Soda Machine - Flowchart

Notice in the second flowchart that there are a couple of times that we may need to repeat a process. You have not seen how to do that in BASIC-256, but it will be covered in the next few chapters.

Exercises:

Word Search

```
z d s y m b o l t r p
e m e w t a f r m r t
y d k c l u a v o s e
p q o z i h p g r p r
x r i c c s r n r e m
z f o w o a i e i t i
a u o c m d x o u s n
q l h m e p u p n q a
f o i q m s t e d u t
b n m h r u s w s b o
g e p r o b l e m p r
```

decision, flowchart, input, output, problem, process, programming, pseudocode, steps, symbol, terminator

Problems

4.1. In complete sentences can you write out the steps to make a peanut butter and jelly sandwich. Assume that the peanut butter jar, jelly jar, loaf of bread, place, and silverware are on the table in front of you. Can another person, who has never seen a PBJ, successfully make one using your directions?

4.2. In a flow chart (or in a similar diagram) diagram the process you go through to open the front door of your hours or apartment. Do you have your keys? Is the door locked? Is it already open?

4.3. In pseudocode (short statements) can you write out directions from your school or work to the nearest restaurant or gas station. Don't cheat and look the directions up on-line. Will the same directions get you back the same way or do the instructions need to be changed?

Chapter 5: Your Program Asks for Advice.

This chapter introduces a new type of variables (string variables) and how to get text and numeric responses from the user.

Another Type of Variable – The String Variable:

In Chapter 3 you got to see numeric variables, which can only store whole or decimal numbers. Sometimes you will want to store a string, text surrounded by quotation marks ("" or "), in the computer's memory. To do this we use a new type of variable called the string variable. A string variable is denoted by appending a dollar sign *$* on a variable name.

You may assign and retrieve values from a string variable the same way you use a numeric variable. Remember, the variable name, case sensitivity, and reserved word rules are the same with string and numeric variables.

```
1    # c5_ilikejim.kbs
2    # I like jim - string variables
3
4    name$ = "Jim"
5    firstmessage$ = '"' + name$ + '" is my friend.'
6    secondmessage$ = "I like " + name$ + "."
7
8    print firstmessage$
9    say firstmessage$
10   print secondmessage$
11   say secondmessage$
```

Program 26: I Like Jim

```
"Jim" is my friend.
```

```
    I like Jim.
```

Sample Output 26: I Like Jim

String variable

A string variable allows you to assign a name to a block of storage in the computer's short-term memory. You may store and retrieve text and character values from the string variable in your program.

A string variable name must begin with a letter; may contain letters and numbers; are case sensitive; and ends with a dollar sign. Also, you can not use words reserved by the BASIC-256 language when naming your variables (see Appendix I). Examples of valid string variable names include: d$, c7$, book$, X$, and barnYard$.

If you assign a numeric value to a string variable, BASIC-256 will convert the number to a string of characters and assign it to the variable.

If you attempt to assign a string to a numeric variable, you will receive a syntax error.

Input – Getting Text or Numbers From the User:

So far we have told the program everything it needs to know in the programming code. The next statement to introduce is *input*. The *input* statement captures either a string or a number that the user types into the text area and stores that value in a variable.

Let's take Program 26 and modify it so that it will ask you for a name and then say hello to that person.

```
1     # c5_ilikeinput.kbs
2     # using input to ask for a name
3
4     input "enter your name>", name$
5     firstmessage$ = name$ + " is my friend."
6     secondmessage$ = "I like " + name$ + "."
7
8     print firstmessage$
9     say firstmessage$
10    print secondmessage$
11    say secondmessage$
```

Program 27: I Like fill in the blank

```
enter your name>Vance
Vance is my friend.
I like Vance.
```

Sample Output 27: I Like fill in the blank

| input *"prompt", stringvariable$* |
| input *"prompt", numericvariable* |
| input *stringvariable$* |
| input *numericvariable* |

New Concept

The **input** statement will retrieve a string or a number that the user types into the text output area of the screen. The result will be stored in a variable that may be used later in the program.

A prompt message, if specified, will display on the text output area and the cursor will directly follow the prompt.

If a numeric result is desired (numeric variable specified in the statement) and the user types a string that can not be converted to a number the input statement will set the variable to zero (0).

The "Math-wiz" program shows an example of input with numeric variables.

```
1     # c5_mathwiz.kbs
2     # show several mathematical operations
3
4     input "a? ", a
5     input "b? ", b
6
7     print a + "+" + b + "=" + (a+b)
8     print a + "-" + b + "=" + (a-b)
9     print b + "-" + a + "=" + (b-a)
10    print a + "*" + b + "=" + (a*b)
11    print a + "/" + b + "=" + (a/b)
12    print b + "/" + a + "=" + (b/a)
```

Program 28: Math-wiz

```
a? 7
b? 56
```

```
7+56=63
7-56=-49
56-7=49
7*56=392
7/56=0.125
56/7=8
```

Sample Output 28: Math-wiz

Big Program

This chapter has two "Big Programs" The first is a fancy program that will say your name and how old you will be in 8 years and the second is a silly story generator.

```
1    # c5_sayname.kbs
2
3    input "What is your name?", name$
4    input "How old are you?", age
5
6    greeting$ =  "It is nice to meet you, " + name$ + "."
7    print greeting$
8    say greeting$
9
10   greeting$ =  "In 8 years you will be " + (age + 8) +
     " years old.  Wow, thats old!"
11   print greeting$
12   say greeting$
```

Program 29: Fancy – Say Name

```
What is your name?Joe
```

```
      How old are you?13
      It is nice to meet you, Joe.
      In 8 years you will be 21 years old.  Wow,
      thats old!
```

Sample Output 29: Fancy – Say Name

```
1      # c5_sillystory.kbs
2
3      print "A Silly Story."
4
5      input "Enter a noun? ", noun1$
6      input "Enter a verb? ", verb1$
7      input "Enter a room in your house? ", room1$
8      input "Enter a verb? ", verb2$
9      input "Enter a noun? ", noun2$
10     input "Enter an adjective? ", adj1$
11     input "Enter a verb? ", verb3$
12     input "Enter a noun? ", noun3$
13     input "Enter Your Name? ", name$
14
15     sentence$ = "A silly story, by " + name$ + "."
16     print sentence$
17     say sentence$
18
19     sentence$ = "One day, not so long ago, I saw a " +
       noun1$ + " " + verb1$ + " down the stairs."
20     print sentence$
21     say sentence$
22
23     sentence$ = "It was going to my " + room1$ + " to " +
       verb2$ + " a " + noun2$
24     print sentence$
25     say sentence$
26
27     sentence$ = "The " + noun1$ + " became " + adj1$ + "
       when I " + verb3$ + " with a " + noun3$ + "."
28     print sentence$
```

```
29      say sentence$
30
31      sentence$ = "The End."
32      print sentence$
33      say sentence$
```

Program 30: Big Program - Silly Story Generator

```
A Silly Story.
Enter a noun? car
Enter a verb? walk
Enter a room in your house? kitchen
Enter a verb? sing
Enter a noun? television
Enter an adjective? huge
Enter a verb? watch
Enter a noun? computer
Enter Your Name? Jim
A silly story, by Jim.
One day, not so long ago, I saw a car walk down
the stairs.
It was going to my kitchen to sing a television
The car became huge when I watch with a
computer.
The End.
```

Sample Output 30: Big Program - Silly Story Generator

Exercises:

Word Search

```
e d l e p g a g j n
p l e a k x l k o g
y r b f b x p e z i
q s o a a h r f l s
q j t m i u i v k r
t s i r p r l w r a
a x f n i t a t g l
h l f y p n y v q l
p w r n i u g x z o
y v c l d z t w v d
```

default, dollarsign, input, prompt, string, variable

Problems

5.1. Write a program to ask for three names. Store them in string variables. Once the user enters the third name have the computer recite the classic playground song using the names:

```
[Name One] and [Name Two]
sitting in a tree,
K-I-S-S-I-N-G.
First comes love,
then comes marriage,
then comes [Name Three]
in a baby carriage!
```

5.2. Write a program to ask for an adjective, noun, animal, and a sound. Once the use enters the last one, build a single string variable (using concatenation) to say a verse of Old MacDonald. Print the result out with a single statement and say it with a single statement. (Adapted from The Old Macdonald Mad Lib from http://www.madglibs.com)

```
           [Adjective] MacDonald had a
           [Noun], E-I-E-I-O and on that
           [Noun] he had an animal, E-I-E-I-O
           with a [Sound] [Sound] here and a
           [Sound] [Sound] there,
           here a [Sound], there a [Sound],
           everywhere a [Sound] [Sound],
           [Adjective] MacDonald had a
           [Noun], E-I-E-I-O.
```

Chapter 6: Decisions, Decisions, Decisions.

The computer is a whiz at comparing things. In this chapter we will explore how to compare two expressions, how to work with complex comparisons, and how to optionally execute statements depending on the results of our comparisons. We will also look at how to generate random numbers.

True and False:

The BASIC-256 language has one more special type of data that can be stored in numeric variables. It is the Boolean data type. Boolean values are either true or false and are usually the result of comparisons and logical operations. Also to make them easier to work with there are two Boolean constants that you can use in expressions, they are: *true* and *false*.

true *false* The two Boolean constants *true* and *false* can be used in any numeric or logical expression but are usually the result of a comparison or logical operator. Actually, the constant *true* is stored as the number one (1) and *false* is stored as the number zero (0).

New Concept

Comparison Operators:

Previously we have discussed the basic arithmetic operators, it is now time to look at some additional operators. We often need to compare two values in a program to help us decide what to do. A comparison operator works with two values and returns true or false based on the result of the comparison.

Operator	Operation
<	Less Than expression1 < expression2 Return true if expression1 is less than expression2, else return false.
<=	Less Than or Equal expression1 <= expression2 Return true if expression1 is less than or equal to expression2, else return false.
>	Greater Than expression1 > expression2 Return true if expression1 is greater than expression2, else return false.
>=	Greater Than or Equal expression1 >= expression2 Return true if expression1 is greater than or equal to expression2, else return false.
=	Equal expression1 = expression2 Return true if expression1 is equal to expression2, else return false.
<>	Not Equal Expression1 <> expression2 Return true if expression1 is not equal to expression2, else return false.

Table 7: Comparison Operators

< <= > >= = <>

The six comparison operations are: less than (<), less than or equal (<=), greater than (>), greater than or equal (>=), equal (=), and not equal (<>). They are used to compare numbers and strings. Strings are compared alphabetically left to right. You may also use parenthesis to group operations together.

New Concept

Making Simple Decisions – The If Statement:

The *if* statement can use the result of a comparison to optionally execute a statement or block of statements. This first program (Program 31) uses three *if* statements to display whether your friend is older, the same age, or younger.

```
1     # c6_compareages.kbs
2     # compare two ages
3
4     input "how old are you?", yourage
5     input "how old is your friend?", friendage
6
7     print "You are ";
8     if yourage < friendage then print "younger than";
9     if yourage = friendage then print "the same age as";
10    if yourage > friendage then print "older than";
11    print " your friend"
```

Program 31: Compare Two Ages

```
how old are you?13
how old is your friend?12
You are older than your friend
```

Sample Output 31: Compare Two Ages

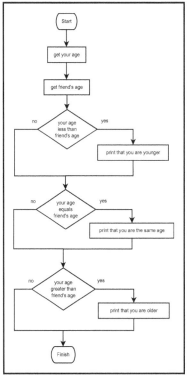

Illustration 16: Compare Two Ages - Flowchart

if *condition* **then** *statement*

If the condition evaluates to *true* then execute the statement
following the *then* clause.

Random Numbers:

When we are developing games and simulations it may become necessary for us to simulate dice rolls, spinners, and other random happenings. BASIC-256 has a built in random number generator to do these things for us.

rand

A random number is returned when rand is used in an expression. The returned number ranges from zero to one, but will never be one ($0 \geq n < 1.0$).

Often you will want to generate an integer from 1 to r, the following statement can be used n = int(rand * r) + 1

int(*number*)
int(*string*)

the **int** function will remove the decimal portion of a number and return just the whole part. No rounding will occur.

Int will also attempt to convert a string to an integer (whole number). If the string does not contain a number then a zero will be returned.

```
1    # c6_coinflip.kbs
2
3    coin = rand
4    if coin < .5 then print "Heads."
5    if coin >= .5 then print "Tails."
```

Program 32: Coin Flip

```
    Tails.
```

Sample Output 32: Coin Flip

<table>
<tr>
<td>
Warning</td>
<td>In program 5.2 you may have been tempted to use the rand expression twice, once in each if statement. This would have created what we call a "Logical Error".

Remember, each time the rand expression is executed it returns a different random number.</td>
</tr>
</table>

Logical Operators:

Sometimes it is necessary to join simple comparisons together. This can be done with the four logical operators: *and*, *or*, *xor*, and *not*. The logical operators work very similarly to the way conjunctions work in the English language, except that "or" is used as one or the other or both.

Operator	Operation
AND	Logical And expression1 AND expression2 If both expression1 and experssion2 are true then return a true value, else return false.

AND		expression1	
		TRUE	**FALSE**
expression2	**TRUE**	TRUE	FALSE
	FALSE	FALSE	FALSE

OR	Logical Or expression1 OR expression2 If either expression1 or experssion2 are true then return a true value, else return false.

OR		expression1	
		TRUE	**FALSE**
expression2	**TRUE**	TRUE	TRUE
	FALSE	TRUE	FALSE

XOR	Logical Exclusive Or expression1 XOR expression2 If only one of the two expressions is true then return a true value, else return false. The XOR operator works like "or" often does in the English language - "You can have your cake xor you can eat it:.

OR		expression1	
		TRUE	**FALSE**
expression2	**TRUE**	FALSE	TRUE
	FALSE	TRUE	FALSE

NOT	Logical Negation (Not) NOT expression1 Return the opposite of expression1. If expression 1 was true then return false. If experssion1 was false then return a true.

NOT		
expression 1	**TRUE**	FALSE
	FALSE	TRUE

and   or   xor   not

The four logical operations: logical and, logical or, logical exclusive or, and logical negation (not) join or modify comparisons. You may also use parenthesis to group operations together.

New Concept

Making Decisions with Complex Results – If/End If:

When we are writing programs it sometimes becomes necessary to do multiple statements when a condition is true. This is done with the alternate format of the *if* statement. With this statement you do not place a statement on the same line as the if, but you place multiple (one or more) statements on lines following the if statement and then close the block of statements with the *end if* statement.

```
if condition then
    statement(s) to execute when true
end if
```

The **if/end if** statements allow you to create a block of programming code to execute when a condition is true. It is often customary to indent the statements with in the **if/end if** statements so they are not confusing to read.

New Concept

```
1    # c6_dice.kbs
2    # roll 2 6-sided dice
3
4    die1 = int(rand * 6) + 1
5    die2 = int(rand * 6) + 1
```

```
6     total = die1 + die2
7
8     print "die 1 = " + die1
9     print "die 2 = " + die2
10    message$ = "You rolled " + total + "."
11
12    if total = 2 then
13       message$ += " Snake eyes."
14    end if
15    if total = 12 then
16       message$ += " Box Cars."
17    end if
18    if die1 = die2 then
19       message$ += " Doubles, roll again!"
20    end if
21
22    print message$
23    say message$
```

Program 33: Rolling Dice

```
die 1 = 6
die 2 = 6
You rolled 12. Box cars. Doubles, roll again!
```

Sample Output 33: Rolling Dice

New Concept

"Edit" then "Beautify" on the menu

The "Beautify" option on the "Edit" menu will clean up the format of your program to make it easier to read. It will remove extra spaces from the beginning and ending of lines and will indent blocks of code (like in the *if/end if* statements).

Deciding Both Ways – If/Else/End If:

The third and last form of the *if* statement is the *if/else/end if*. This extends the if/end if statements by allowing you to create a block of code to execute if the condition is true and another block to execute when the condition is false.

New Concept

```
if condition then
      statement(s) to execute when true
else
      statement(s) to execute when false
end if
```

The **if**, **else**, and **end if** statements allow you to define two blocks of programming code. The first block, after the **then** clause, executes if the condition is true and the second block, after the **else** clause, will execute when the condition if false.

Program 34 re-writes Program 32 using the *else* statement.

```
1    # c6_coinflip2.kbs
2    # coin flip with else
3
4    coin = rand
5    if coin < .5 then
6        print "Heads."
7        say "Heads."
8    else
9        print "Tails."
10       say "Tails."
11   end if
```

Program 34: Coin Flip – With Else

```
Heads.
```

Sample Output 34: Coin Flip – With Else

Nesting Decisions:

One last thing. With the *if/end if* and the *if/else/end if* statements it is possible to nest an *if* inside the code of another. This can become confusing but you will see this happening in future chapters.

Big Program

This chapter's big program is a program to roll a single 6-sided die and then draw on the graphics display the number of dots.

```
1    # c6_dieroll.kbs
2    # roll a 6-sided die on the screen
3
4    # hw - height and width of the dots on the dice
5    hw = 70
6    # margin - space before each dot
7    #   1/4 of the space left over after we draw 3 dots
8    margin = (300 - (3 * hw)) / 4
9    # z1 - x and y position of top of top row and column
     of dots
10   z1 = margin
11   # z2 - x and y position of top of middle row and
     column of dots
12   z2 = z1 + hw + margin
13   # z3 - x and y position of top of bottom row and
     column of dots
14   z3 = z2 + hw + margin
```

```
15
16    # get roll
17    roll = int(rand * 6) + 1
18
19    color black
20    rect 0,0,300,300
21
22    color white
23    # top row
24    if roll <> 1 then rect z1,z1,hw,hw
25    if roll = 6 then rect z2,z1,hw,hw
26    if roll >= 4 and roll <= 6 then rect z3,z1,hw,hw
27    # middle
28    if roll = 1 or roll = 3 or roll = 5 then rect
      z2,z2,hw,hw
29    # bottom row
30    if roll >= 4 and roll <= 6 then rect z1,z3,hw,hw
31    if roll = 6 then rect z2,z3,hw,hw
32    if roll <> 1 then rect z3,z3,hw,hw
33
34    message$ = "You rolled a " + roll + "."
35    print message$
36    say message$
```

Program 35: Big Program - Roll a Die and Draw It

Sample Output 35: Big Program - Roll a Die and Draw It

Exercises:

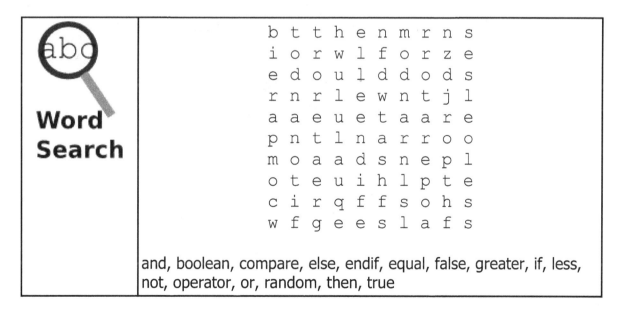

Word Search

```
b t t h e n m r n s
i o r w l f o r z e
e d o u l d d o d s
r n r l e w n t j l
a a e u e t a a r e
p n t l n a r r o o
m o a a d s n e p l
o t e u i h l p t e
c i r q f f s o h s
w f g e e s l a f s
```

and, boolean, compare, else, endif, equal, false, greater, if, less, not, operator, or, random, then, true

Problems

6.1. Write a program that will toss a coin and tell you if your guess was correct. Assign a variable with a random number. Ask the user to enter the letter 'h' or 't' (for heads or tails). If the number is less than .5 and the user entered 'h' or the number was greater than or equal .5 and the user chose 't' then tell them they won the toss.

6.2. Modify program #6.1 to also tell the user that they did not win the toss.

6.3. Write a simple program to draw a round of rock, paper, scissors. Use two numeric variables and assign a draw (random number) to each one. If a variable is less than 1/3 then it will be rock, greater than or equal to 1/3 and less than 2/3 it will be paper, and 2/3 or greater it will be scissors. Display what the two draws are.

6.4. Take the simple rock,paper,scissors draw program from #6.3 and add rules to say who won. Remember "paper covers rock", "rock smashes scissors", and "scissors cut paper". If both players draw the same thing then declare the round a "draw".

6.5. Take the rock paper scissors game from #6.4 and add graphics and sound. Draw paper as a white rectangle, rock as a darkorange circle, and scissors as a red X. Have the computer announce the winner.

Chapter 7: Looping and Counting - Do it Again and Again.

So far our program has started, gone step by step through our instructions, and quit. While this is OK for simple programs, most programs will have tasks that need to be repeated, things counted, or both. This chapter will show you the three looping statements, how to speed up your graphics, and how to slow the program down.

The For Loop:

The most common loop is the *for* loop. The *for* loop repeatedly executes a block of statements a specified number of times, and keeps track of the count. The count can begin at any number, end at any number, and can step by any increment. Program 36 shows a simple for statement used to say the numbers 1 to 10 (inclusively). Program 37 will count by 2 starting at zero and ending at 10.

```
1    # c7_for.kbs
2    for t = 1 to 10
3       print t
4       say t
5    next t
```

Program 36: For Statement

```
1
2
3
4
5
6
7
```

```
        8
        9
        10
```

Sample Output 36: For Statement

```
1        # c7_forstep2.kbs
2        for t = 0 to 10 step 2
3            print t
4             say t
5        next t
```

Program 37: For Statement – With Step

```
        0
        2
        4
        6
        8
        10
```

Sample Output 37: For Statement – With Step

```
for variable = expr1 to expr2 [step expr3]
      statement(s)
next variable
```

Execute a specified block of code a specified number of times. The *variable* will begin with the value of *expr1*. The *variable* will be incremented by *expr3* (or one if step is not specified) the second and subsequent time through the loop. Loop terminates if *variable* exceeds *expr2*.

Using a loop we can easily draw very interesting graphics. Program 38 will draw a Moiré Pattern. This really interesting graphic effect is caused by the computer being unable to draw perfectly straight lines. What is actually drawn are pixels in a stair step fashion to approximate a straight line. If you look closely at the lines we have drawn you can see that they actually are jagged.

```
1    # c7_moire.kbs
2    # draw a moire pattern
3
4    clg
5    color black
6    for t = 1 to 300 step 3
7        line 0,0,300,t
8        line 0,0,t,300
9    next t
```

Program 38: Moiré Pattern

Sample Output 38: Moiré Pattern

Explore

What kind of Moiré Patterns can you draw? Start in the center, use different step values, overlay one on top of another, try different colors, go crazy.

For statements can even be used to count backwards. To do this set the step to a negative number.

```
1    # c7_stepneg1.kbs
2
3    for t = 10 to 0 step -1
4       print t
```

```
5           pause 1.0
6       next t
```

Program 39: For Statement – Countdown

```
10
9
8
7
6
5
4
3
2
1
0
```

Sample Output 39: For Statement – Countdown

 **New Concept**	**pause** *seconds* The pause statement tells BASIC-256 to stop executing the current program for a specified number of seconds. The number of seconds may be a decimal number if a fractional second pause is required.

Do Something Until I Tell You To Stop:

The next type of loop is the *do/until*. The *do/until* repeats a block of code one or more times. At the end of each iteration a logical condition is tested. The loop repeats as long as the condition is *false*. Program 40 uses the do/until loop to repeat until the user enters a number from 1 to 10.

```
1    # c7_dountil.kbs
2
3    do
4        input "enter a number from 1 to 10?",n
5    until n>=1 and n<=10
6    print "you entered " + n
```

Program 40: Get a Number from 1 to 10

```
enter a number from 1 to 10?66
enter a number from 1 to 10?-56
enter a number from 1 to 10?3
you entered 3
```

Sample Output 40: Get a Number from 1 to 10

do
statement(s)
until *condition*
Do the statements in the block over and over again while the condition is false.
The statements will be executed **one or more times**.

New Concept

Do Something While I Tell You To Do It:

The third type of loop is the *while/end while*. It tests a condition before executing each iteration and if it evaluates to true then executes the code in the loop. The *while/end while* loop may execute the code inside the loop zero or more times.

Sometimes we will want a program to loop forever, until the user stops the program. This can easily be accomplished using the Boolean *true* constant (see Program 41).

```
1    # c7_whiletrue.kbs
2
3    while true
4        print "nevermore ";
5    end while
```

Program 41: Loop Forever

```
nevermore.
nevermore.
nevermore.
nevermore.
nevermore.
... runs until you stop it
```

Sample Output 41: Loop Forever

New Concept	`while condition`
	`    statement(s)`
	`end while`
	
	Do the statements in the block over and over again while the condition is true.
	
	The statements will be executed **zero or more times**.

Program 42 uses a while loop to count from 1 to 10 like Program 36 did with a *for* statement.

```
1       # c7_whilefor.kbs
2
3       t = 1
4       while t <= 10
5          print t
6          t = t + 1
7       end while
```

Program 42: While Count to 10

```
1
2
3
4
5
6
7
8
9
10
```

Sample Output 42: While Count to 10

Continuing and Exiting Loops

Sometimes it becomes necessary for a programmer to jump out of a loop before it would normally terminate (exit) or to start the next loop (continue) without executing all of the code.

```
8       # adding machine
1       # c7_exitwhile.kbs
2
3       total = 0
```

```
4     while true
5         input "Enter Value (-999 to exit) > ", v
6         if v = -999 then exit while
7         total = total + v
8     end while
9
10    print "Your total was " + total
```

Program 43: Adding Machine - Using Exit While

```
Enter Value (-999 to exit) > 34
Enter Value (-999 to exit) > -34
Enter Value (-999 to exit) > 234
Enter Value (-999 to exit) > 44
Enter Value (-999 to exit) > -999
Your total was 278
```

Sample Output 43: Adding Machine - Using Exit While

New Concept

```
exit do
exit for
exit while
```

Jump out of the current loop and skip the remaining code in the loop.

```
continue do
continue for
continue while
```

Do not execute the rest of the code in this loop but loop again like normal.

New Concept

Fast Graphics:

When we need to execute many graphics quickly, like with animations or games, BASIC-256 offers us a fast graphics system. To turn on this mode you execute the *fastgraphics* statement. Once *fastgraphics* mode is started the graphics output will only be updated once you execute the *refresh* statement.

```
fastgraphics
refresh
```

Start the **fastgraphics** mode. In fast graphics the screen will only be updated when the **refresh** statement is executed.

New Concept

Once a program executes the **fastgraphics** statement it can not return to the standard graphics (slow) mode.

```
1    # c7_kaleidoscope.kbs
2
3    clg
4    fastgraphics
5    for t = 1 to 100
6        r = int(rand * 256)
```

```
7          g = int(rand * 256)
8          b = int(rand * 256)
9          x = int(rand * 300)
10         y = int(rand * 300)
11         h = int(rand * 100)
12         w = int(rand * 100)
13         color rgb(r,g,b)
14         rect x,y,w,h
15         rect 300-x-w,y,w,h
16         rect x,300-y-h,w,h
17         rect 300-x-w,300-y-h,w,h
18      next t
19      refresh
```

Program 44: Kaleidoscope

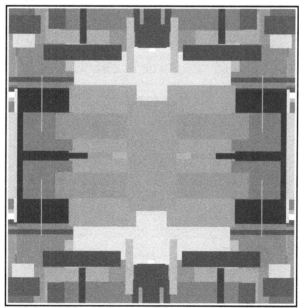

Sample Output 44: Kaleidoscope

Big Program

In this chapter's "Big Program" let's use a while loop to animate a ball bouncing around on the graphics display area.

```
1    # c7_bouncingball.kbs
2
3    fastgraphics
4    clg
5
6    # starting position of ball
7    x = rand * 300
8    y = rand * 300
9    # size of ball
10   r = 10
11   # speed in x and y directions
12   dx = rand * r + 2
13   dy = rand * r + 2
14
15   color green
16   rect 0,0,300,300
17
18   while true
19      # erase old ball
20      color white
21      circle x,y,r
22      # calculate new position
23      x = x + dx
24      y = y + dy
25      # if off the edges turn the ball around
26      if x < 0 or x > 300 then
27         dx = dx * -1
28         sound 1000,50
```

```
29       end if
30       # if off the top or bottom turn the ball around
31       if y < 0 or y > 300 then
32          dy = dy * -1
33          sound 1500,50
34       end if
35       # draw new ball
36       color red
37       circle x,y,r
38       # update the display
39       refresh
40    end while
```

Program 45: Big Program - Bouncing Ball

Sample Output 45: Big Program - Bouncing Ball

Exercises:

Word Search

```
f l g b w p e t s w i i
f a w t b q l i t n u i
t n s n v h p h b c f e
i a k t c v r o o e l l
x d r k g e w n o i l c
e x o u f r d e h l o i
i g f r y i a w l n l c
t x e n t g d p t i w k
g s d i o n e i h p h a
h w o a e d n z m i g w
x n s d z u u d w t c d
x o m i e h d g m o v s
```

condition, continue, do, endwhile, exit, fastgraphics, for, loop, next, refresh, step, until, while

Problems

7.1. Write a program that uses the **for** loop to sum the integers from 1 to 42 and display the answer. Hint: before the loop assign a variable to zero to accumulate the total.

7.2. Write a program that asks the user for an integer from 2 to 12 in a loop. Keep looping until the user enters a number in the range. Calculate the factorial (n!) of the number using a **for** loop and display it. Remember 2! is 1*2, 3! is 1*2*3, and n! Is n * (n-1)!.

7.3. Write a program to display one through 8 multiplied by 1 through 8. Hint: use a **for** loop inside another **for** loop. Format your output to look like:

```
1 * 1 = 1
1 * 2 = 2
1 * 3 = 3
1 * 4 = 4
1 * 5 = 5
1 * 6 = 6
1 * 7 = 7
1 * 8 = 8
2 * 1 = 2
2 * 2 = 4
2 * 3 = 6
...
```

7.4. Re-write #7.3 to make your output in table format, like:

```
1  2  3  4  5  6  7  8
2  4  6  8 10 12 14 16
3  6  9 12 15 18 21 24
4  8 12 16 20 24 28 32
5 10 15 20 25 30 35 40
6 12 18 24 30 36 42 48
7 14 21 28 35 42 49 56
8 16 24 32 40 48 56 64
```

Chapter 8: Custom Graphics – Creating Your Own Shapes.

This chapter we will show you how to draw colorful words and special shapes on your graphics window. Several topics will be covered, including: fancy text; drawing polygons on the graphics output area; and stamps, where we can position, re-size, and rotate polygons. You also will be introduced to angles and how to measure them in radians.

Fancy Text for Graphics Output:

You have been introduced to the *print* statement (Chapter 1) and can output strings and numbers to the text output area. The *text* and *font* statements allow you to place numbers and text on the graphics output area in a variety of styles.

```
1    # c8_graphichello.kbs
2    # drawing text
3
4    clg
5    color red
6    font "Tahoma",33,100
7    text 100,100,"Hello."
8    font "Impact",33,50
9    text 100,150,"Hello."
10   font "Courier New",33,50
11   text 100,250,"Hello."
```

Program 46: Hello on the Graphics Output Area

Sample Output 46: Hello on the Graphics Output Area

New Concept

`text x, y, expression`

Draw the contents of the *expression* on the graphics output area with it's top left corner specified by *x* and *y*. Use the font, size, and weight specified in the last **font** statement.

New Concept

`font font_name, size_in_point, weight`

Set the font, size, and weight for the next *text* statement to use to render text on the graphics output area.

Argument	Description
font_name	String containing the system font name to use. A font must be previously loaded in the system before it may be used. Common font names under Windows include: "Verdana", "Courier New", "Tahoma", "Arial", and "Times New Roman".
size_in_point	Height of text to be rendered in a measurement known as point. There are 72 points in an inch.
weight	Number from 1 to 100 representing how dark letter should be. Use 25 for light, 50 for normal, and 75 for bold.

Microsoft Sans Serif   Impact

Verdana   Times New Roman

Courier New   **Arial Black**

Tahoma   Georgia

Arial   Palatino Linotype

Trebuchet MS   **Century Gothic**

Comic Sans MS   *Monotype Corsiva*

Lucida Console   French Script MT

Illustration 17: Common Windows Fonts

Resizing the Graphics Output Area:

By default the graphics output area is 300x300 pixels. While this is sufficient for many programs, it may be too large or too small for others. The graphsize statement will re-size the graphics output area to what ever custom size you require. Your program may also use the graphwidth and graphheight functions to see what the current graphics size is set to.

```
1    # c8_resizegraphics.kbs
2    # resize the graphics output area
3
4    graphsize 500,500
5    xcenter = graphwidth/2
6    ycenter = graphheight/2
7
8    color black
9    line xcenter, ycenter - 10, xcenter, ycenter + 10
10   line xcenter - 10, ycenter, xcenter + 10, ycenter
11
12   font "Tahoma",12,50
13   text xcenter + 10, ycenter + 10, "Center at (" +
     xcenter + "," + ycenter + ")"
```

Program 47: Re-size Graphics

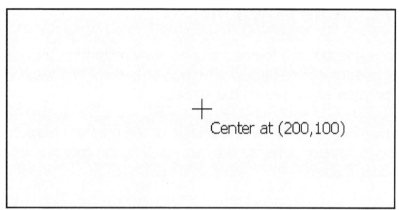

Center at (200,100)

Sample Output 47: Re-size Graphics

New Concept

`graphsize` *width*, *height*

Set the graphics output area to the specified *height* and *width*.

New Concept

`graphwidth` or `graphwidth()`
`graphheight` or `graphheight()`

Functions that return the current graphics height and width for you to use in your program.

Creating a Custom Polygon:

In previous chapters we learned how to draw rectangles and circles. Often we want to draw other shapes. The *poly* statement will allow us to draw a custom polygon anywhere on the screen.

Let's draw a big red arrow in the middle of the graphics output area. First, draw it on a piece of paper so we can visualize the coordinates of the vertices of the arrow shape.

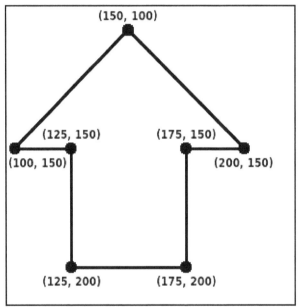

Illustration 18: Big Red Arrow

Now start at the top of the arrow going clockwise and write down the x and y values.

```
1     # c8_bigredarrow.kbs
2     clg
3     color red
```

```
4      poly {150, 100, 200, 150, 175, 150, 175, 200, 125,
       200, 125, 150, 100, 150}
```

Program 48: Big Red Arrow

Sample Output 48: Big Red Arrow

New Concept

```
poly {x1, y1, x2, y2 ...}
poly numeric_array
```

Draw a polygon.

Stamping a Polygon:

The *poly* statement allowed us to place a polygon at a specific location on the screen but it would be difficult to move it around or adjust it. These problems are solved with the *stamp* statement. The stamp statement takes a location on the screen, optional scaling (re-sizing), optional rotation, and a polygon definition to allow us to place a polygon anywhere we want it in the screen.

Let's draw an equilateral triangle (all sides are the same length) on a piece of paper. Put the point (0,0) at the top and make each leg 10 units long (see Illustration 19).

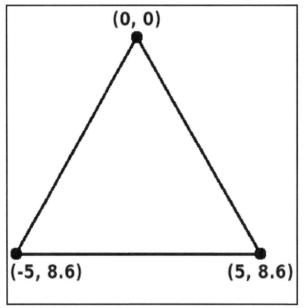

Illustration 19: Equilateral Triangle

Now we will create a program, using the simplest form of the *stamp* statement, to fill the screen with triangles. Program 49 Will do just that. It uses the triangle stamp inside two nested loops to fill the screen.

```
1    # c8_stamptriangle.kbs
2    # use a stamp to draw many triangles
3
4    clg
5    color black
6    for x = 25 to 200 step 25
7       for y = 25 to 200 step 25
8          stamp x, y, {0, 0, 5, 8.6, -5, 8.6}
9       next y
10   next x
```

Program 49: Fill Screen with Triangles

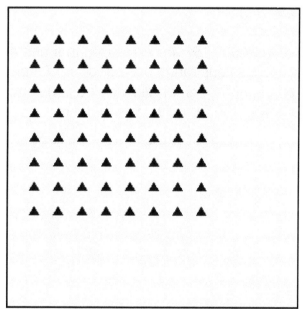

Sample Output 49: Fill Screen with Triangles

```
stamp x, y, {x1, y1, x2, y2 ...}
stamp x, y, numeric_array
stamp x, y, scale, {x1, y1, x2, y2 ...}
stamp x, y, scale, numeric_array
stamp x, y, scale, rotate, {x1, y1, x2, y2 ...}
stamp x, y, scale, rotate, numeric_array
```

New Concept

Draw a polygon with it's origin (0,0) at the screen position (x,y). Optionally scale (re-size) it by the decimal scale where 1 is full size. Also you may also rotate the stamp clockwise around it's origin by specifying how far to rotate as an angle expressed in radians (0 to 2π).

New Concept

Radians 0 to 2π

Angles in BASIC-256 are expressed in a unit of measure known as a radian. Radians range from 0 to 2π. A right angle is π/2 radians and an about face is π radians. You can convert degrees to radians with the formula $r = d/180 * \pi$.

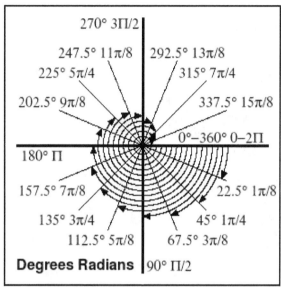

Illustration 20: Degrees and Radians

Let's look at another example of the stamp program. Program 50 used the same isosceles triangle as the last program but places 100 of them at random locations, randomly scaled, and randomly rotated on the screen.

```
1    # c8_stamptriangle2.kbs
2    # stamp randomly sized and rotated triangles
3
4    clg
5    color black
6    for t = 1 to 100
7      x = rand * graphwidth
8      y = rand * graphheight
9      s = rand * 7          # scale up to 7 times larger
10     r = rand * 2 * pi     # rotate up to 2pi (360
    degrees)
11     stamp x, y, s, r, {0, 0, 5, 8.6, -5, 8.6}
12   next t
```

Program 50: One Hundred Random Triangles

Sample Output 50: One Hundred Random Triangles

`pi`

The constant *pi* can be used in expressions so that you do not have to remember the value of π. Π is approximately 3.1415.

New Concept

Sixteen Million Different Colors

BASIC-256 will allow you to define up to 16,777,216 unique colors when you draw. The RGB color model adds red (R), green (G), and blue (B) light together to form new colors. If all of the three colors are set to zero the color Black will be created, if All three colors are set to the maximum value of 255 then the color will be white.

```
1    # c8_512colors.kbs
2    # show a few of the 16 million colors
3    graphsize 256, 256
4    clg
5
6    for r = 0 to 255 step 32
7        for g = 0 to 255 step 32
8            for b = 0 to 255 step 32
9                color rgb(r,g,b)
10               rect b/8+g, r, 4, 32
11           next b
12       next g
13
14   next r
```

Program 51: 512 colors of the 16 million

Sample Output 51: 512 colors of the 16 million

rgb(*red*, *green*, *blue*)
rgb(*red*, *green*, *blue*, *alpha*)

The **rgb** function returns a single number that represents a color expressed by the three or four values. The *red, blue,* and *green* values represent how much of those colors to include (255-on to 0-off). The optional alpha value represents how transparent the color is (255-solid to 0-totally transparent).

```
15    # c8_stamptriangle3.kbs
16    # stamp randomly colored, sized and rotated triangles
17
18    clg
19    penwidth 3
20
21    for t = 1 to 100
22       x = rand * graphwidth
23       y = rand * graphheight
24       s = rand * 7          # scale up to 7 times larger
25       r = rand * 2 * pi     # rotate up to 2pi (360
      degrees)
26       rpen = rand * 256      # get the RGBparts of a
      random pen color
27       gpen = rand * 256
28       bpen = rand * 256
29       rbrush = rand * 256   # random brush (fill) color
30       gbrush = rand * 256
31       bbrush = rand * 256
32       color rgb(rpen, gpen, bpen), rgb(rbrush, gbrush,
      bbrush)
33       stamp x, y, s, r, {0, 0, 5, 8.6, -5, 8.6}
34    next t
```

Program 52: 100 Random Triangles with Random Colors

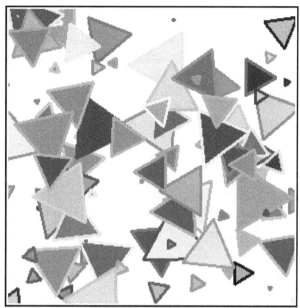

Sample Output 52: 100 Random Triangles with Random Colors

In addition to setting the exact color we want we can also define a color to be transparent. The RGB function has a fourth optional argument to set the alpha (transparency) property of a color. Zero is totally see through, and invisible, while 255 is totally opaque.

```
1    # c8_transparent.kbs
2    # show the nature of transparent colors
3    clg
4
5    color rgb(255,0,0,127)
6    circle 100,100,100
7
8    color rgb(0,255,0,127)
9    circle 200,100,100
10
11   color rgb(0,0,255,127)
12   circle 100,200,100
13
```

```
14      color rgb(0,0,0,127)
15      circle 200,200,100
```

Program 53: Transparent Circles

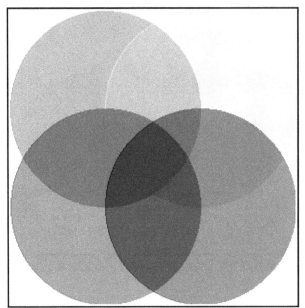

Sample Output 53: Transparent Circles

```
1       # c8_stamptriangle4.kbs
2       # stamp randomly colored, sized and rotated triangles
3
4       clg
5       penwidth 3
6
7       for t = 1 to 100
8          x = rand * graphwidth
9          y = rand * graphheight
10         s = rand * 7          # scale up to 7 times larger
11         r = rand * 2 * pi     # rotate up to 2pi (360
        degrees)
12         rpen = rand * 256     # get the RGBparts of a
        random pen color
13         gpen = rand * 256
```

```
14        bpen = rand * 256
15        apen = rand * 256
16        rbrush = rand * 256   # random brush (fill) color
17        gbrush = rand * 256
18        bbrush = rand * 256
19        abrush = rand * 256
20        color rgb(rpen, gpen, bpen, apen), rgb(rbrush,
       gbrush, bbrush, abrush)
21        stamp x, y, s, r, {0, 0, 5, 8.6, -5, 8.6}
22    next t
```

Program 54: 100 Random Triangles with Random Transparent Colors

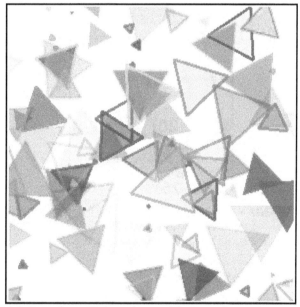

Sample Output 54: 100 Random Triangles with Random Transparent Colors

Big Program

Let's send flowers to somebody special. The following program draws a flower using rotation and a stamp.

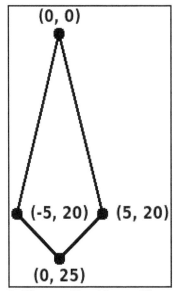

Illustration 21: Big Program - A Flower For You - Flower Petal Stamp

```
1     # c8_aflowerforyou.kbs
2     # use stamps to draw a flower
3
4     clg
5
6     color green
7     rect 148,150,4,150
8
9     color rgb(255,128,128)
10    for r = 0 to 2*pi step pi/4
```

```
11        stamp graphwidth/2, graphheight/2, 2, r, {0, 0, 5,
          20, 0, 25, -5, 20}
12   next r
13
14   color rgb(128,128,255)
15   for r = 0 to 2*pi step pi/5
16        stamp graphwidth/2, graphheight/2, 1, r, {0, 0, 5,
          20, 0, 25, -5, 20}
17   next r
18
19   message$ = "A flower for you."
20
21   color darkyellow
22   font "Tahoma", 14, 50
23   text 10, 10, message$
24   say message$
```

Program 55: Big Program - A Flower For You

Sample Output 55: Big Program - A Flower For You

Exercises:

Word Search

```
t n e r a p s n a r t j
k c r l s e u l b h e s
v g p r t r z a g c c g
b h d x a r x i t i f r
a s e m s d e f h g w a
p t e t f h i p p r i p
a o a e h o a a f e t h
e m i p r r n r n e h s
p w a n g g e t q n g i
l r u o t d e u u j i z
g r a p h w i d t h e e
s i p o l y g o n c w f
```

alpha, blue, degrees, font, graphheight, graphics, graphsize, graphwidth, green, pi, point, polygon, radian, red, rgb, stamp, text, transparent, weight

Problems

8.1. Use two **poly** and one **rect** statements to draw a simple house similar to the one shown below. Your house can be any combination of colors you wish it to be.

Use the hexagon below as a guide to help you to solve Problems 8.2 through 8.4. The sides of the hexagon are one unit long and the origin (0,0) is in the center of the shape.

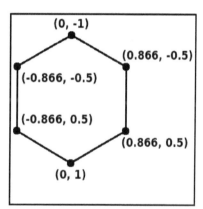

8.2. Use a **color** statement with a clear brush and a single **poly** statement to draw a hexagon in the center of the graphics screen with each side 100 pixels long.

8.3. Rewrite #8.2 to use a **stamp** statement. Use the scale feature of stamp so that you may draw a hexagon of any size by only changing one number.

8.4. Put the **stamp** statement from #8.3 inside a **for** loop and draw a series of nested hexagons by changing the scale. You may want to experiment with the step clause and with rotating the hexagon at the same time.

Chapter 9: Functions and Subroutines – Reusing Code.

This chapter introduces the use of Functions and Subroutines. Programmers create subroutines and functions to test small parts of a program, reuse these parts where they are needed, extend the programming language, and simplify programs.

Functions:

A function is a small program within your larger program that does something for you. You may send zero or more values to a function and the function will return one value. You are already familiar with several built in functions like: **rand** and **rgb**. Now we will create our own.

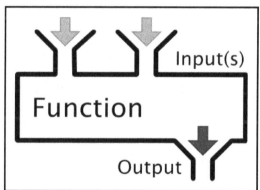

Illustration 22: Block Diagram of a Function

New Concept

```
Function functionname( argument(s) )
    statements
End Function

Function functionname$( argument(s) )
    statements
End Function
```

The **Function** statement creates a new named block of programming statements and assigns a unique name to that block of code. It is recommended that you do not name your function the same name as a variable in your program, as it may cause confusion later.

In the required parenthesis you may also define a list of variables that will receive values from the "calling" part of the program. These variables belong to the function and are not available to the part of the program that calls the function.

A function definition must be closed or finished with an **End Function**. This tells the computer that we are done defining the function.

The value being returned by the function may be set in one of two ways: 1) by using the **return** statement with a value following it or 2) by setting the function name to a value within the function.

New Concept

Return value

Execute the **return** statement within a function to return a value and send control back to where it was called from.

New Concept

end

Terminates the program (stop).

```
1     # c9_minimum.kbs
2     # minimum function
3
4     input "enter a number ", a
5     input "enter a second number ", b
6
7     print "the smaller one is ";
8     print minimum(a,b)
9     end
10
11    function minimum(x,y)
12    # return the smallest of the two numbers passed
13       if x<y then return x
14       return y
15    end function
```

Program 56: Minimum Function

```
enter a number 7
enter a second number 3
the smaller one is 3
```

Sample Output 56: Minimum Function

```
1      # c9_gameroller.kbs
2      # Game Dice Roller
3
4      print "die roller"
5      s = get("sides on the die",6)
6      n = get("number of die", 2)
7      total = 0
8      for x = 1 to n
9         d = die(s)
10        print d
11        total = total + d
12     next x
13     print "total "+ total
14     end
15
16     function get(message$, default)
17        # get a number - if they enter zero
18        # or enter default to another value
19        input message$ + " (default " + default + ") ?", n
20        if n = 0 then n = default
21        return n
22     end function
23
24     function die(sides)
25        # roll a die and return 1 to sides
26        return int(rand*sides)+1
27     end function
```

Program 57: Game Dice Roller

```
die roller
sides on the die (default 6) ?6
number of die (default 2) ?3
6
3
1
total 10
```

Sample Output 57: Game Dice Roller

In the examples above we have created functions that returned a numeric value. Functions may also be created that return a string value. A string function, like a variable, has a dollar sign after its name to specify that is returns a string.

```
1      # c9_repeatstring.kbs
2      # simple string function - make copies
3
4      a$ = "hi"
5      b$ = repeat$(a$,20)
6      print a$
7      print b$
8      end
9
10     function repeat$(w$,n)
11         a$ = ""
12         for t = 1 to n
13             a$ += w$
14         next t
15         return a$
16     end function
```

Program 58: Simple String Function

```
hi
hihihihihihihihihihihihihihihihihihihihi
```

Sample Output 58: Simple String Function

Observe in the function samples, above, that variables within a function exist only within the function. If the same variable name is used in the function it DOES NOT change the value outside the function.

Subroutines:

A subroutine is a small subprogram within your larger program that does something specific. Subroutines allow for a single block of code to be used by different parts of a larger program. A subroutine may have values sent to it to tell the subroutine how to react.

Subroutines are like functions except that they do not return a value and that they require the use of the **call** statement to execute them.

New Concept

```
Subroutine subroutinename( argument(s) )
    statements
End Subroutine
```

The **Subroutine** statement creates a new named block of programming statements and assigns a unique name to that block of code. It is recommended that you do not name your subroutine the same name as a variable in your program, as it may cause confusion later.

In the required parenthesis you may also define a list of variables that will receive values from the "calling" part of the program. These variables are local to the subroutine and are not directly available to the calling program.

A subroutine definition must be closed or finished with an **End Subroutine**. This tells the computer that we are done defining the subroutine.

Call subroutinename(value(s))

The **Call** statement tells BASIC-256 to transfer program control to the subroutine and pass the values to the subroutine for processing.

New Concept

Return

Execute the **return** statement within a subroutine to send control back to where it was called from.

This version of the return statement does not include a value to return, as a subroutine does not return a value.

New Concept

```
1    # c9_subroutineclock.kbs
2    # display a comple ticking clock
3
4    fastgraphics
5    font "Tahoma", 20, 100
6    color blue
7    rect 0, 0, 300, 300
8    color yellow
9    text 0, 0, "My Clock."
10
11   while true
12      call displaytime()
13      pause 1.0
14   end while
15
16   end
```

```
17
18    subroutine displaytime()
19       color blue
20       rect 100, 100, 200, 100
21       color yellow
22       text 100, 100, hour + ":" + minute + ":" + second
23       refresh
24    end subroutine
```

Program 59: Subroutine Clock

Sample Output 59: Subroutine Clock

```
hour   or hour()
minute or minute()
second   or second()
month or month()
day  or day()
year or year()
```

New Concept

The functions **year**, **month**, **day**, **hour**, **minute**, and **second** return the components of the system clock. They allow your program to tell what time it is.

year	Returns the system 4 digit year.
month	Returns month number 0 to 11. 0 – January, 1- February...
day	Returns the day of the month 1 to 28,29,30, or 31.
hour	Returns the hour 0 to 23 in 24 hour format. 0 – 12 AM, 1- 1 AM, ... 12 – 12 PM, 13 – 1 PM, 23 – 11 PM ...
minute	Returns the minute 0 to 59 in the current hour.
second	Returns the second 0 to 59 in the current minute.

```
1    # c9_subroutineclockimproved.kbs
2    # better ticking clock
3
4    fastgraphics
5    font "Tahoma", 20, 100
6    color blue
7    rect 0, 0, 300, 300
8
9    call displayyear()
10   while true
11      call displaytime()
12      pause 1.0
```

```
13     end while
14
15     end
16
17     subroutine displayyear()
18        color blue
19        rect 50,50, 200, 100
20        color yellow
21        text 50,50, padnumber$(month) + "/" + padnumber$
       (day) + "/" + padnumber$(year)
22        refresh
23     end subroutine
24
25     subroutine displaytime()
26        color blue
27        rect 50,100, 200, 100
28        color yellow
29        text 50, 100, padnumber$(hour) + ":" + padnumber$
       (minute) + ":" + padnumber$(second)
30        refresh
31     end subroutine
32
33     function padnumber$(n)
34        padnumber$ = string(n)
35        if n < 10 then
36           padnumber$ = "0" + padnumber$
37        end if
38     end function
```

Program 60: Subroutine Clock - Improved

Sample Output: 60: Subroutine Clock - Improved

Using the Same Code in Multiple Programs:

Once a programmer creates a subroutine or function they may want to re-use these blocks of code in other programs. You may copy and paste the code from one program to another but what if you want to make small changes and want the change made to all of your programs. This is where the **include** statement comes in handy.

The include statement tells BASIC-256 at compile time (when you first press the run button) to bring in code from other files. In Program 61 (below) you can see that the functions have been saved out as their own files and included back into the main program.

```
1    # c9_gamerollerinclude.kbs
2    # Game Dice Roller
3
4    include "e2_c9_diefunction.kbs"
5    include "e2_c9_inputnumberfunction.kbs"
6
7    print "die roller"
8    s = inputnumber("sides on the die",6)
9    n = inputnumber("number of die", 2)
10   total = 0
11   for x = 1 to n
12   d = die(s)
13   print d
```

```
14      total = total + d
15      next x
16      print "total "+ total
17      end
```

Program 61: Game Dice Roller – With Included Functions

```
1       # c9_diefunction.kbs
2       # function to roll a N sided die
3
4       function die(sides)
5       # roll a die and return 1 to sides
6       return int(rand*sides)+1
7       end function
```

Program 62: Game Dice Roller – die Function

```
1       # c9_inputnumberfunction.kbs
2
3       function inputnumber(prompt$, default)
4       # get a number - if they enter zero
5       # or enter default to another value
6       input prompt$ + " (default " + default + ") ?", n
7       if n = 0 then n = default
8       return n
9       end function
```

Program 63: Game Dice Roller – inputnumber Function

Now that we have split out the functions we can use them in different programs, without having to change the function code or re-typing it.

```
1       # c9_addingmachine.kbs
2       # create a nice adding machine
```

```
3
4        include "e2_c9_inputnumberfunction.kbs"
5
6        print "adding machine"
7        print "press stop to end"
8
9        total = 0
10       while true
11       a = inputnumber("+ ",0)
12       total = total + a
13       print total
14       end while
```

Program 64: Adding Machine – Using the inputnumber Function

```
adding machine
press stop to end
+ (default 0) ?6
6
+ (default 0) ?
6
+ (default 0) ?55
61
+ (default 0) ?
```

Sample Output 64: Adding Machine – Using the inputnumber Function

include "string constant"

Include code from an external file at compile (when run is clicked).

The file name must be in quotes and can not be a variable or other expression.

New Concept

Labels, Goto, and Gosub:

This section contains a discussion of labels and how to cause your program to jump to them. These methods are how we used to do it before subroutines and functions were added to the language. ***These statements can be used to create ugly and overly complex programs and should be avoided.***

In Program 41 Loop Forever we saw an example of looping forever. This can also be done using a label and a *goto* statement.

```
1    # c9_goto.kbs
2    top:
3    print "hi"
4    goto top
```

Program 65: Goto With a Label

```
hi
hi
hi
hi
... repeats forever
```

Sample Output 65: Goto With a Label

label:

A label allows you to name a place in your program so you may jump to that location later in the program. You may have multiple labels in a single program, but each label can only exist in one place.

A label name is followed with a colon (:); must be on a line with no other statements; must begin with a letter; may contain letters and numbers; and are case sensitive. Also, you can not use words reserved by the BASIC-256 language when naming labels (see Appendix I), or the names of subroutines and functions.

Examples of valid labels include: top:, far999:, and About:.

New Concept

goto label

The **goto** statement causes the execution to jump to the statement directly following the label.

New Concept

Subroutines and functions allow us to reuse blocks of code. The gosub statement also allows a programmer to reuse code. Variables in a gosub block are global to the entire program.

Program 66 shows an example of a subroutine that is called three times.

```
1    # c9_gosub.kbs
2    # a simple gosub
3
```

```
4      a = 10
5      for t = 1 to 3
6         print "a equals " + a
7         gosub showline
8      next t
9      end
10
11     showline:
12     print "------------------"
13     a = a * 2
14     return
```

Program 66: Gosub

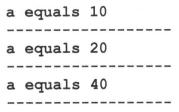

```
a equals 10
------------------
a equals 20
------------------
a equals 40
------------------
```

Sample Output 66: Gosub

gosub *label*

The **gosub** statement causes the execution to jump to the subroutine defined by the *label*.

New Concept

Big Program

In our "Big Program" this chapter, let's make a program to roll two dice, draw them on the screen, and give the total. Let's use an included function to generate the random number of spots and a subroutine to draw the image so that we only have to write it once.

```
1    # c9_roll2dice2.kbs
2    # roll two dice graphically
3
4    include "e2_c9_diefunction.kbs"
5
6    clg
7    total = 0
8
9    roll = die(6)
10   total = total + roll
11   call drawdie(30,30, roll)
12
13   roll = die(6)
14   total = total + roll
15   call drawdie(130,130, roll)
16
17   print "you rolled " + total + "."
18   end
19
20   subroutine drawdie(x,y,n)
21   # set x,y for top left and n for number of dots
22   # draw 70x70 with dots 10x10 pixels
23   color black
24   rect x,y,70,70
25   color white
26   # top row
27   if n <> 1 then rect x + 10, y + 10, 10, 10
28   if n = 6 then rect x + 30, y + 10, 10, 10
```

```
29      if n >= 4 and n <= 6 then rect x + 50, y + 10, 10, 10
30      # middle
31      if n = 1 or n = 3 or n = 5 then rect x + 30, y + 30,
        10, 10
32      # bottom row
33      if n >= 4 and n <= 6 then rect x + 10, y + 50, 10, 10
34      if n = 6 then rect x + 30, y + 50, 10, 10
35      if n <> 1 then rect x + 50, y + 50, 10, 10
36      end subroutine
```

Program 67: Big Program - Roll Two Dice Graphically

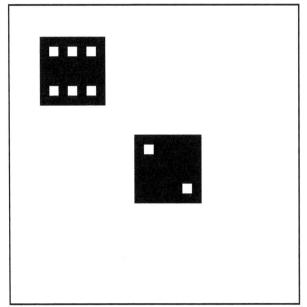

Sample Output 67: Big Program - Roll Two Dice Graphically

Exercises:

Word Search

```
g o t o d e j j v e q y
k x a w r n x d s q a n
u i d r x i o p i d r o
l n h r g t z c s c e i
k c l e p u j d e p t t
g l e t a o m n h s a c
o u b u l r h e t v n n
s d a r l b f r n h i u
u e l n a u i a e t m f
b m z j c s l e r n r n
e t u n i m e y a o e b
h o u r s o w w p m t n
```

argument, call, day, end, file, function, gosub, goto, hour, include, label, minute, month, parenthesis, return, second, subroutine, terminate, year

Problems

9.1. Create a subroutine that will accept two numbers representing a point on the screen. Have the routine draw a smiling face with a radius of 20 pixels at that point. You may use circles, rectangles, or polygons as needed. Call that subroutine in a loop 100 times and draw the smiling faces at random locations to fill the screen.

9.2. Write a program that asks for two points x1, y1 and x2, y2 and displays the formula for the line connecting those two points in slope-intercept format ($y=mx+b$). Create a function that returns the slope (m) of the connecting line using the formula $\frac{y1-y2}{x1-x2}$. Create a second function that returns the y intercept (b) when the x and y coordinates of one of the points and the slope are passed to the function.

```
x1? 1
y1? 1
x2? 3
y2? 2
y = 0.5x + 0.5
```

9.3. In mathematics the term factorial means the product of consecutive numbers and is represented by the exclamation point. The symbol n! means n * (n-1) * (n-2) * ... * 3 * 2 * 1 where n is an integer and 0! is 1 by definition.

Write a function that accepts one number and returns its factorial. Call that new function within a for loop to display 1! to 10!. Your output should look like:

```
1!  is  1
2!  is  2
3!  is  6
4!  is  24
5!  is  120
6!  is  720
7!  is  5040
8!  is  40320
9!  is  362880
10!  is  3628800
```

9.4. A recursive function is a special type of function that calls itself. Knowing that n! = n * (n-1)! and that 0! = 1 rewrite #9.3 to use a recursive function to calculate a factorial.

Chapter 10: Mouse Control – Moving Things Around.

This chapter will show you how to make your program respond to a mouse. There are two different ways to use the mouse: tracking mode and clicking mode. Both are discussed with sample programs.

Tracking Mode:

In mouse tracking mode, there are three numeric functions (**mousex**, **mousey**, and **mouseb**) that will return the coordinates of the mouse pointer over the graphics output area. If the mouse is not over the graphics display area then the mouse movements will not be recorded (the last location will be returned).

```
1    # c10_mousetrack.kbs
2    # track the mouse with a circle
3
4    print "Move the mouse around the graphics window."
5    print "Click left mouse button to quit."
6
7    fastgraphics
8
9    # do it over and over until the user clicks left
10   while mouseb <> 1
11     # erase screen
12     color white
13     rect 0, 0, graphwidth, graphheight
14     # draw new ball
15     color red
16     circle mousex, mousey, 10
17     refresh
18   end while
```

```
19
20    print "all done."
21    end
```

Program 68: Mouse Tracking

Sample Output 68: Mouse Tracking

New Concept

```
mousex or mousex()
mousey or mousey()
mouseb or mouseb()
```

The three mouse functions will return the current location of the mouse as it is moved over the graphics display area. Any mouse motions outside the graphics display area are not recorded, but the last known coordinates will be returned.

mousex	Returns the x coordinate of the mouse pointer position. Ranges from 0 to **graphwidth** -1.	
mousey	Returns the y coordinate of the mouse pointer position. Ranges from 0 to **graphheight** -1.	
mouseb	0	Returns this value when no mouse button is being pressed.
	1	Returns this value when the "left" mouse button is being pressed.
	2	Returns this value when the "right" mouse button is being pressed.
	4	Returns this value when the "center" mouse button is being pressed.
	If multiple mouse buttons are being pressed at the same time then the value returned will be the button values added together.	

Clicking Mode:

The second mode for mouse control is called "Clicking Mode". In clicking mode, the mouse location and the button (or combination of buttons) are stored when the click happens. Once a click is processed by the program a *clickclear* command can be executed to reset the click, so the next one can be recorded.

```
1    # c10_mouseclick.kbs
2    # X marks the spot where you click
3
4    print "Move the mouse around the graphics window"
5    print "click left mouse button to mark your spot"
6    print "click right mouse button to stop."
7    clg
8    clickclear
9    while clickb <> 2
10      # clear out last click and
11      # wait for the user to click a button
12      clickclear
13      while clickb = 0
14        pause .01
15      end while
16      #
17      color blue
18      stamp clickx, clicky, 5, {-1, -2, 0, -1, 1, -2, 2,
     -1, 1, 0, 2, 1, 1, 2, 0, 1, -1, 2, -2, 1, -1, 0, -2,
     -1}
19   end while
20   print "all done."
21   end
```

Program 69: Mouse Clicking

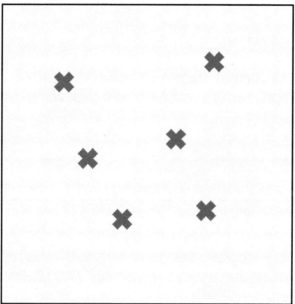

Sample Output 69: Mouse Clicking

New Concept

```
clickx   or clickx()
clicky   or clicky()
clickb or clickb()
```

The values of the three click functions are updated each time a mouse button is clicked when the pointer is on the graphics output area. The last location of the mouse when the last click was received are available from these three functions.

clickclear

The **clickclear** statement resets the **clickx**, **clicky**, and **clickb** functions to zero so that a new click will register when **clickb** <> 0.

New Concept

Big Program

The big program this chapter uses the mouse to move color sliders so that we can see all 16,777,216 different colors on the screen.

```
1    # c10_colorchooser.kbs
2    fastgraphics
3
4    print "colorchooser - find a color"
5    print "click and drag red, green and blue sliders"
6
7    # variables to store the color parts
8    r = 128
9    g = 128
10   b = 128
11
12   call display(r,g,b)
13
14   while true
15      # wait for click
16      while mouseb = 0
17         pause .01
```

```
18          end while
19          # change color sliders
20          # the red slider y range is 0 >= red < 75
21          if mousey < 75 then
22             r = mousex
23             if r > 255 then r = 255
24          end if
25          # the green slider y range is 75 >= red < 150
26          if mousey >= 75 and mousey < 150 then
27             g = mousex
28             if g > 255 then g = 255
29          end if
30          # the blue slider y range is 150 >= red < 225
31          if mousey >= 150 and mousey < 225 then
32             b = mousex
33             if b > 255 then b = 255
34          end if
35          call display(r,g,b)
36       end while
37       end
38
39       subroutine colorline(r,g,b,x,y)
40          # draw part of the color bar the color r,g,b from
         x,y to x,y+37
41          color rgb(r, g, b)
42          line x, y, x, y+37
43       end subroutine
44
45       subroutine redsliderbar(r,g,b)
46          # draw the red bar from 0,0 to 255,74
47          font "Tahoma", 30, 100
48          color rgb(255, 0, 0)
49          text 260, 10, "r"
50          for t = 0 to 255
51             # red and red hues
52             call colorline(t, 0, 0, t, 0)
53             call colorline(t, g, b, t, 38)
54          next t
55          color black
```

```
56      rect r-1, 0, 3, 75
57   end subroutine
58
59   subroutine greensliderbar(r,g,b)
60      # draw thegreen bar from 0,75 to 255,149
61      font "Tahoma", 30, 100
62      color rgb(0, 255, 0)
63      text 260, 85, "g"
64      for t = 0 to 255
65         # green and green hues
66         call colorline(0, t, 0, t, 75)
67         call colorline(r, t, b, t, 113)
68      next t
69      # slider
70      color black
71      rect g-1, 75, 3, 75
72   end subroutine
73
74   subroutine bluesliderbar(r,g,b)
75      # draw the blue bar from 0,150 to 255,224
76      font "Tahoma", 30, 100
77      color rgb(0, 0, 255)
78      text 260, 160, "b"
79      for t = 0 to 255
80         # blue and blue hues
81         call colorline(0, 0, t, t, 150)
82         call colorline(r, g, t, t, 188)
83      next t
84      # slider
85      color black
86      rect b-1, 150, 3, 75
87   end subroutine
88
89   subroutine display(r, g, b)
90      clg
91      call redsliderbar(r,g,b)
92      call greensliderbar(r,g,b)
93      call bluesliderbar(r,g,b)
94      # draw swatch
```

```
95        color black
96        font "Tahoma", 13, 100
97        text 5, 235, "(" + r + "," + g + "," + b + ")"
98        color rgb(r,g,b)
99        rect 151,226,150,75
100       refresh
101    end subroutine
```

Program 70: Big Program - Color Chooser

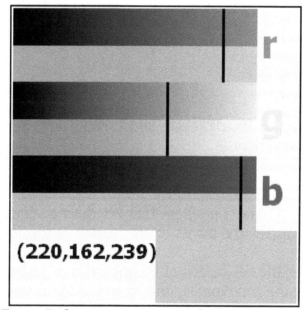

Sample Output 70: Error: Reference source not found

Exercises:

Word Search

```
r f m t x v t x n j
j a a o h k s f o u
n c e y u t c l e c
b e x l e s h i y l
k n z m c s e w l i
c t m o r k u b k c
i e z u n i c o g k
l r p s g s g i m y
c j i e h w l h l m
c x l x m f z a t c
```

center, clickb, clickclear, clickx, clicky, left, mouseb, mousex, mousey, right

---

Problems

10.1. Create a program that will draw a series of connected lines and display the points on the screen as the lines are drawn.

When the left button of the mouse is clicked draw a small circle, print the coordinates, draw a line to the previous coordinates (if not the first point), and remember the point so that it can be the start of the next line. Repeat this until the user clicks stop.

```
46,62
187,59
178,132
108,96
```

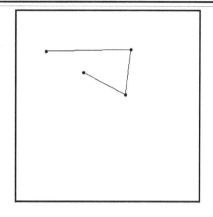

10.2. Create a program that will allow the user to use the mouse like a paintbrush. When the user has the left button depressed then plot a point at that location. To make the line wider you may draw a circle with a radius of 2 or 3.

For extra skill when the user presses the right button make the pen color a random color

10.3. Use the smiling face subroutine from Problem 9.1 to make a mouse drawing program with the smile. When the user clicks on a point of the screen draw a face there.

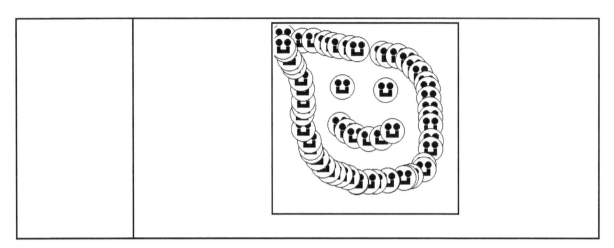

Chapter 11: Keyboard Control – Using the Keyboard to Do Things.

This chapter will show you how to make your program respond to the user when a key is pressed (arrows, letters, and special keys) on the keyboard.

Getting the Last Key Press:

The *key* function returns the last raw keyboard code generated by the system when a key was pressed. Certain keys (like control-c and function-1) are captured by the BASIC256 window and will not be returned by key. After the last key press value has been returned the function value will be set to zero (0) until another keyboard key has been pressed.

The key values for printable characters (0-9, symbols, letters) are the same as their upper case Unicode values regardless of the status of the caps-lock or shift keys.

```
1    # c11_readkey.kbs
2    print "press a key - Q to quit"
3    do
4       k = key
5       if k <> 0 then
6          if k >=32 and k <= 127 then
7             print chr(k) + "=";
8          end if
9          print k
10      end if
11   until k = asc("Q")
12   end
```

Program 71: Read Keyboard

```
press a key - Q to quit
A=65
Z=90
M=77
16777248
&=38
7=55
```

Sample Output 71: Read Keyboard

key
key()

The **key** function returns the value of the last keyboard key the user has pressed. Once the key value is read by the function, it is set to zero to denote that no key has been pressed.

New Concept

Unicode

The Unicode standard was created to assign numeric values to letters or characters for the world's writing systems. There are more than 107,000 different characters defined in the Unicode 5.0 standard.

New Concept See: http://www.unicode.org

`asc(expression)`

The **asc** function returns an integer representing the Unicode value of the first character of the string *expression*.

`chr(expression)`

The **chr** function returns a string, containing a single character with the Unicode value of the integer *expression*.

Another example of a key press program would be a program to display a letter and to time the user to see how long it took them to press the letter on the keyboard. This program also introduces the **msec** statement that returns the number of milliseconds (1/1000 of a second) that the program has been running.

```
1    # c11_msec.kbs
2
3    # get the code for a random character from A-Z
4    c = asc("A") + int(rand*26)
5
6    # display the letter (from the numeric code)
7    print "press '" + chr(c) + "'"
8
9    time = msec    # get the start time
```

```
10    do           # wait for the key
11       k = key
12    until k = c
13    time = msec - time  # calculate how long
14
15    print "it took you " + (time/1000) + " seconds to
      find that letter."
```

Program 72: Keyboard Speed Drill

```
press 'C'
it took you 1.833 seconds to find that letter.
```

Sample Output 72: Keyboard Speed Drill

New Concept

msec()
msec

The **msec** function returns the length of time that a program has been running in milliseconds (1/1000 of a second).

How about we look at a more complex example? Program 73 Draws a red ball on the screen and the user can move it around using the keyboard.

```
1    # c11_moveball.kbs
2    # move a ball on the screen with the keyboard
3
4    print "use i for up, j for left, k for right, m for
     down, q to quit"
5
```

```
6     fastgraphics
7     clg
8
9     # position of the ball
10    # start in the center of the screen
11    x = graphwidth /2
12    y = graphheight / 2
13    r = 20  # size of the ball (radius)
14
15    # draw the ball initially on the screen
16    call drawball(x, y, r)
17
18    # loop and wait for the user to press a key
19    while true
20       k = key
21       if k = asc("I") then
22          y = y - r
23          if y < r then y = graphheight - r
24          call drawball(x, y, r)
25       end if
26       if k = asc("J") then
27          x = x - r
28          if x < r then x = graphwidth - r
29          call drawball(x, y, r)
30       end if
31       if k = asc("K") then
32          x = x + r
33          if x > graphwidth - r then x = r
34          call drawball(x, y, r)
35       end if
36       if k = asc("M") then
37          y = y + r
38          if y > graphheight - r then y = r
39          call drawball(x, y, r)
40       end if
41       if k = asc("Q") then exit while
42    end while
43    print "all done."
44    end
```

```
45
46   subroutine drawball(ballx, bally, ballr)
47      color white
48      rect 0, 0, graphwidth, graphheight
49      color red
50      circle ballx, bally, ballr
51      refresh
52   end subroutine
```

Program 73: Move Ball

Sample Output 73: Move Ball

Big Program

The big program this chapter is a game using the keyboard. Random letters are going to fall down the screen and you score points by pressing the key as fast as you can.

```
1    # c11_fallinglettergame.kbs
2
3    speed = .15 # drop speed - lower to make faster
4    nletters = 10 # letters to play
5
6    score = 0
7    misses = 0
8    color black
9
10   fastgraphics
11
12   clg
13   font "Tahoma", 20, 50
14   text 20, 80, "Falling Letter Game"
15   font "Tahoma", 16, 50
16   text 20, 140, "Press Any Key to Start"
17   refresh
18   # clear keyboard and wait for any key to be pressed
19   k = key
20   while key = 0
21      pause speed
22   end while
23
24   misses = nletters # assume they missed everything
25   for n = 1 to nletters
26      letter = int((rand * 26)) + asc("A")
27      x = 10 + rand * 225
28      for y = 0 to 250 step 20
29         clg
30         # show letter
31         font "Tahoma", 20, 50
32         text x, y, chr(letter)
33         # show score and points
34         font "Tahoma", 12, 50
35         value = (250 - y)
36         text 10, 270, "Value "+ value
37         text 200, 270, "Score "+ score
38         refresh
```

```
39              k = key
40              if k <> 0 then
41                 if k = letter then
42                    score = score + value
43                    misses-- # didnt miss this one
44                 else
45                    score = score - value
46                 end if
47                 exit for
48              end if
49              pause speed
50           next y
51     next n
52
53     clg
54     font "Tahoma", 20, 50
55     text 20, 40, "Falling Letter Game"
56     text 20, 80, "Game Over"
57     text 20, 120, "Score: " + score
58     text 20, 160, "Misses: " + misses
59     refresh
60     end
```

Program 74: Big Program - Falling Letter Game

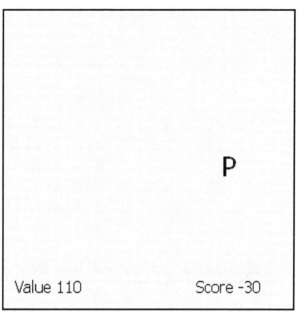

Sample Output 74: Big Program - Falling Letter Game

Exercises:

Word Search

```
k g c v f k e t
e a o w y c o u
y b n o h o z n
t b t r b l n i
f u r r t s g c
i t o a t p y o
h j l m e a b d
s i c s a c j e
```

arrow, asc, capslock, chr, control, key, shift, unicode

Problems

11.1. Take Program 72: Keyboard Speed Drill from this chapter and modify it to display ten letters, one at a time, and wait for the user to press that key. Once the user has pressed the correct letters display the total time it took the user.

As an added challenge add logic to count the number of errors and allow a user to retry a letter until they successfully type it.

```
press 'A'
press 'M'
press 'O'
error
press 'U'
press 'X'
press 'V'
press 'K'
press 'C'
press 'Z'
press 'Z'
it took you 15.372 seconds to find
```

```
them.
you made 1 errors.
```

11.2. Create a graphical game like "whack-a-mole" that displays a number on the screen and will wait a random length of time (try 0.5 to 1.5 seconds) for the user to press that number. If they do play a happy sound and display the next, if they miss it or are not fast enough play a sad sound. When they have missed 5 then show them how many they were able to get.

11.3. Create a piano program using the keys of your keyboard. Wait in a loop so that when the user presses a key the program will play a sound for a short period of time. Assign keys on the keyboard frequencies that correspond to notes on Illustration 10 found on page 42.

Chapter 12: Images, WAVs, and Sprites

This chapter will introduce the really advanced multimedia and graphical statements. Saving images to a file, loading them back, playing sounds from WAV files, and really cool animation using sprites.

Saving Images to a File:

So far we have seen how to create shapes and graphics using the built in drawing statements. The **imgsave** statement allows you to save your images to one of many standard image formats.

Program 75 Draws a series of pentagons, each a little bigger and rotated to make a beautiful geometric flower. It would be nice to use that image somewhere else. This program creates a PNG (Portable Network Graphics) file that can be used on a Web site, presentation, or anywhere else you may want to use it.

```
1    # c12_5pointed.kbs
2    #
3    graphsize 100,100
4    clg
5    color black,clear
6    for s = 1 to 50 step 2
7    stamp 50,50,s,s,{0,-1, .95,-.31, .59,.81, -.59,.81,
     -.95,-.31}
8    next s
9    #
10   imgsave "c12_5pointed.png"
```

Program 75: Save an Image

Sample Output 75: Save an Image

New Concept

```
imgsave filename
imgsave filename, type
```

Save the current graphics output to an image file. If the type is not specified the graphic will be saved as a Portable Network Graphic (PNG) file. You may optionally save the image as a "BMP" or "JPG" type file by specifying the type as a second argument.

Images From a File:

The **imgload** statement allows you to load a picture from a file and display it in your BASIC-256 programs. These images can be ones you have saved yourself or pictures from other sources.

```
1    # c12_imgloadball.kbs
2    # load an image from a file
3
4    clg
5    for i = 1 to 50
6        imgload rand * graphwidth, rand * graphheight,
     "greenball.png"
7    next i
```

Program 76: Imgload a Graphic

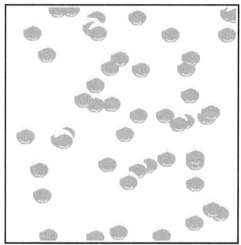

Sample Output 76: Imgload a Graphic

Program 76 Shows an example of this statement in action. The last argument is the name of a file on your computer. It needs to be in the same folder as the program, unless you specify a full path to it. Also notice that the coordinates (x,y) represent the CENTER of the loaded image and not the top left corner.

Warning

Most of the time you will want to save the program into the same folder that the image or sound file is in BEFORE you run the program. This will set your current working directory so that BASIC-256 can find the file to load.

New Concept

```
imgload x, y, filename
imgload x, y, scale, filename
imgload x, y, scale, rotation, filename
```

Read in the picture found in the file and display it on the graphics output area. The values of x and y represent the location to place the CENTER of the image.

Images may be loaded from many different file formats, including: BMP, PNG, GIF, JPG, and JPEG.

Optionally scale (re-size) it by the decimal scale where 1 is full size. Also you may also rotate the image clockwise around it's center by specifying how far to rotate as an angle expressed in radians (0 to 2π).

The **imgload** statement also allows optional scaling and rotation like the **stamp** statement does. Look at Program 77 for an example.

```
1    # c12_imgloadpicasso.kbs
2    # show img with rotation and scaling
3    # photo from
     http://i988.photobucket.com/albums/af3/fikarvista/pic
     asso_selfport1907.jpg
4
5    graphsize 500,500
6    clg
7    for i = 1 to 50
8        imgload graphwidth/2, graphheight/2, i/50,
     2*pi*i/50, "picasso_selfport1907.jpg"
9    next i
10   say "hello Picasso."
```

Program 77: Imgload a Graphic with Scaling and Rotation

Sample Output 77: Imgload a Graphic with Scaling and Rotation

Playing Sounds From a WAV file:

So far we have explored making sounds and music using the **sound** command and text to speech with the **say** statement. BASIC-256 will also play sounds stored in WAV files. The playback of a sound from a WAV file will happen in the background. Once the sound starts the program will continue to the next statement and the sound will continue to play.

```
1    # c12_numberpopper.kbs
2    # wav files from
     http://www.grsites.com/archive/sounds/
3
4    fastgraphics
5    wavplay "cartoon002.wav"
6
```

```
7      speed = .05
8      for t = 1 to 3
9         n = int(rand * 6 + 1)
10        for pt = 1 to 200 step 10
11           font "Tahoma",pt,100
12           clg
13           color black
14           text 10,10, n
15           refresh
16           pause speed
17        next pt
18        speed = speed / 2
19     next t
20     # wait for sound to complete
21     wavwait
22
23     wavplay "people055.wav"
24     wavwait
25     end
```

Program 78: Popping Numbers with Sound Effects

New Concept

```
wavplay filename
wavplay ( filename )
wavwait
wavstop
```

The **wavplay** statement loads a wave audio file (.wav) from the current working folder and plays it. The playback will be synchronous meaning that the next statement in the program will begin immediately as soon as the audio begins playing.

Wavstop will cause the currently playing wave audio file to stop the synchronous playback and **wavwait** will cause the program to stop and wait for the currently playing sound to complete.

Moving Images - Sprites:

Sprites are special graphical objects that can be moved around the screen without having to redraw the entire screen. In addition to being mobile you can detect when one sprite overlaps (collides) with another. Sprites make programming complex games and animations much easier.

```
1    # c12_sprite1ball.kbs
2    # sounds from
     http://www.freesound.org/people/NoiseCollector
3
4    color white
5    rect 0, 0, graphwidth, graphheight
6
7    spritedim 1
8
9    spriteload 0, "blueball.png"
10   spriteplace 0, 100,100
11   spriteshow 0
12
13   dx = rand * 10
14   dy = rand * 10
15
16   while true
17     if spritex(0) <=0 or spritex(0) >= graphwidth -1
     then
18         dx = dx * -1
19         wavplay "4359__NoiseCollector__PongBlipF4.wav"
20       end if
21     if spritey(0) <= 0 or spritey(0) >= graphheight -1
     then
22         dy = dy * -1
23         wavplay "4361__NoiseCollector__pongblipA_3.wav"
24       endif
25     spritemove 0, dx, dy
26     pause .05
27   end while
```

Program 79: Bounce a Ball with Sprite and Sound Effects

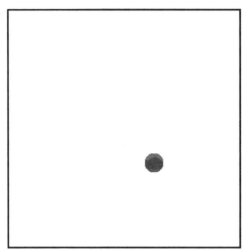

Sample Output 79: Bounce a Ball with Sprite and Sound Effects

As you can see in Program 79 the code to make a ball bounce around the screen, with sound effects, is much easier than earlier programs to do this type of animation. When using sprites we must tell BASIC-256 how many there will be (**spritedim**), we need to set them up (**spriteload** , **spritepoly**, or **spriteplace**), make them visible (**spriteshow**), and then move them around (**spritemove**). In addition to these statements there are functions that will tell us where the sprite is on the screen (**spritex** and **spritey**), how big the sprite is (**spritew** and **spriteh**) and if the sprite is visible (**spritev**).

New Concept

```
spritedim numberofsprites
spritedim ( numberofsprites )
```

The **spritedim** statement initializes, or allocates in memory, places to store the specified number of sprites. You may allocate as many sprites as your program may require but your program may slow down if you create too many sprites.

New Concept

```
spriteload spritenumber, filename
spriteload ( spritenumber, filename )
```

This statement reads an image file (GIF, BMP, PNG, JPG, or JPEG) from the specified path and creates a sprite.

By default the sprite will be placed with its center at 0,0 and it will be hidden. You should move the sprite to the desired position on the screen (**spritemove** or **spriteplace**) and then show it (**spriteshow**).

New Concept

```
spritehide spritenumber
spritehide ( spritenumber )

spriteshow spritenumber
spriteshow ( spritenumber )
```

The **spriteshow** statement causes a loaded, created, or hidden sprite to be displayed on the graphics output area.

Spritehide will cause the specified sprite to not be drawn on the screen. It will still exist and may be shown again later.

New Concept

```
spriteplace spritenumber, x, y
spriteplace ( spritenumber, x, y )
```

The **spriteplace** statement allows you to place a sprite's center at a specific location on the graphics output area.

New Concept

```
spritemove spritenumber, dx, dy
spritemove ( spritenumber, dx, dy )
```

Move the specified sprite *x* pixels to the right and *y* pixels down. Negative numbers can also be specified to move the sprite left and up.

A sprite's center will not move beyond the edge of the current graphics output window (0,0) to (**graphwidth**-1, **graphheight**-1).

You may move a hidden sprite but it will not be displayed until you show the sprite using the **showsprite** statement.

New Concept

```
spritev(spritenumber)
```

This function returns a true value if a loaded sprite is currently displayed on the graphics output area. False will be returned if it is not visible.

New Concept

	spriteh(*spritenumber*) spritew(*spritenumber*) spritex(*spritenumber*) spritey(*spritenumber*)

These functions return various pieces of information about a loaded sprite.

spriteh	Returns the height of a sprite in pixels.
spritew	Returns the width of a sprite in pixels.
spritex	Returns the position on the x axis of the center of the sprite.
spritey	Returns the position on the y axis of the center of the sprite.

The second sprite example (Program 80) we now have two sprites. The first one (number zero) is stationary and the second one (number one) will bounce off of the walls and the stationary sprite.

```
1    # c12_spritebumper.kbs
2    # show two sprites with collision
3
4    color white
5    rect 0, 0, graphwidth, graphheight
6
7    spritedim 2
8
9    # stationary bumber
10   spriteload 0, "paddle.png"
11   spriteplace 0,graphwidth/2,graphheight/2
12   spriteshow 0
13
14   # moving ball
```

```
15      spriteload 1, "greenball.png"
16      spriteplace 1, 50, 50
17      spriteshow 1
18      dx = rand * 5 + 5
19      dy = rand * 5 + 5
20
21      while true
22          if spritex(1) <=0 or spritex(1) >= graphwidth -1
        then
23              dx = dx * -1
24          end if
25          if spritey(1) <= 0 or spritey(1) >= graphheight -1
        then
26              dy = dy * -1
27          end if
28          if spritecollide(0,1) then
29              dy = dy * -1
30              print "bump"
31          end if
32          spritemove 1, dx, dy
33          pause .05
34      end while
```

Program 80: Two Sprites with Collision

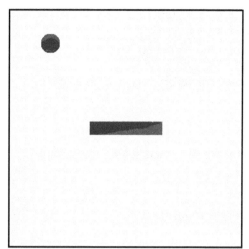

Sample Output 80: Two Sprites with Collision

New Concept

`spritecollide(spritenumber1, spritenumber2)`

This function returns true of the two sprites collide with or overlap each other.

Sprites may also be created using a polygon as seen in Chapter 8: Custom Graphics – Creating Your Own Shapes. This is accomplished using the **spritepoly** statement.

```
1       # c12_spritepoly.kbs
2       # create a sprite from a polygon
3       # that follows the mouse
4
5       spritedim 1
6       color red, blue
7       penwidth 1
```

```
8      spritepoly 0, {15,0, 30,10, 20,10, 20,30, 10,30,
       10,10, 0,10}
9
10     color green
11     rect 0,0,graphwidth, graphheight
12
13     spriteshow 0
14     while true
15        spriteplace 0, mousex, mousey
16        pause .01
17     end while
```

Program 81: Creating a Sprite From a Polygon

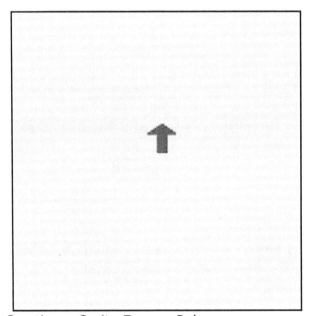

Sample Output 81: Creating a Sprite From a Polygon

New Concept

```
spritepoly spritenumber, { points }
spritepoly ( spritenumber, { points } )

spritepoly spritenumber, array_variable
spritepoly ( spritenumber, array_variable )
```

Create a new sprite from the list of points defining a polygon. The top left corner of the polygon should be in the position 0,0 and the sprite's size will be automatically created.

Big Program

The "Big Program" for this chapter uses sprites and sounds to create a paddle ball game.

```
1    # c12_sprite_paddleball.kbs
2    # paddleball game made with sprites
3    # sounds from
     http://www.freesound.org/people/NoiseCollector
4
5    print "paddleball game"
6    print "J and K keys move the paddle"
7    input "Press enter to start >", wait$
8
9    color white
10   rect 0, 0, graphwidth, graphheight
11
12   spritedim 2
13   color blue, darkblue
14   spritepoly 0, {0,0, 80,0, 80,20, 70,20, 70,10, 10,10,
     10,20, 0,20}
```

```
15     spriteplace 0, 100,270
16     spriteshow 0
17     spriteload 1, "greenball.png"
18     spriteplace 1, 100,100
19     spriteshow 1
20     penwidth 2
21
22     dx = rand * .5 + .25
23     dy = rand * .5 + .25
24
25     bounces = 0
26
27     while spritey(1) + spriteh(1) - 5 < spritey(0)
28        k = key
29        if chr(k) = "K" then
30           spritemove 0, 20, 0
31        end if
32        if chr(k) = "J" then
33           spritemove 0, -20, 0
34        end if
35        if spritecollide(0,1) then
36           # bounce back ans speed up
37           dy = dy * -1
38           dx = dx * 1.1
39           bounces = bounces + 1
40           wavstop
41           wavplay "96633__CGEffex__Ricochet_metal5.wav"
42           # move sprite away from paddle
43           while spritecollide(0,1)
44              spritemove 1, dx, dy
45           end while
46        end if
47        if spritex(1) <=0 or spritex(1) >= graphwidth -1
       then
48           dx = dx * -1
49           wavstop
50           wavplay "4359__NoiseCollector__PongBlipF4.wav"
51        end if
52        if spritey(1) <= 0 then
```

```
53          dy = dy * -1
54          wavstop
55          wavplay "4361__NoiseCollector__pongblipA_3.wav"
56       end if
57       spritemove 1, dx, dy
58       # adjust the speed here
59       pause .002
60    end while
61
62    print "You bounced the ball " + bounces + " times."
```

Program 82: Paddleball with Sprites

Sample Output 82: Paddleball with Sprites

Exercises:

Word Search

```
i s d d i m e n s i o n o z u
s e j i e s c a l e h e w d w
k p v c i r z n r o y d a s o
z j r p m a u o z l u i v p h
a e m i t s t t o m e l w r s
c f v f t a m p c c l l a i e
q o h o t e e i a i g o i t t
w j l i m t l l d w p c t e i
q a o l i e p o a e f e w h r
w n v r i e t v a i t t j i p
q b p p t s s i m d h i s d s
o s v i l t i a r m t r r e c
u u r w o a g o y p s r p z
h p a p g e y a n d s s e f s
s f t s b k i m g l o a d u o
```

collision, dimension, image, imgload, picture, rotation, scale, spritecollide, spritedim, spritehide, spriteload, spritemove, spriteplace, spritepoly, spriteshow, wavplay, wavstop, wavwait

Problems

12.1. Write a program to draw a coin, on a graphics window that is 100x100 pixels with a face on it. Save the image as "head.png". Have the same program erase the screen, draw the back side of the coin, and save it as "tail.png". Make the coins your own design.

12.2. Now write a simple coin toss program that displays the results of a coin toss using the images created in program 12.1. Generate a random number and test if the number is less than .5 then show the heads image otherwise show the tails image.

For an extra challenge make random heads and tails appear on the screen until the user presses a key.

12.3. Use a program like "Audacity" to record two WAV audio files, one with your voice saying "heads" and the other saying "tails". Add these audio files to the program you wrote in 12.2.

12.4. Type in and modify Program 82: Paddleball with Sprites to create a two player "ping-pong" type game. You will need to add a third sprite for the "top" player and assign two keys to move their paddle.

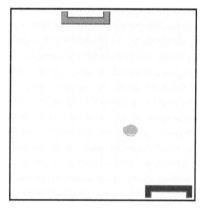

Chapter 13: Printing

With BASIC-256 you can create output and send it to a printer or to a PDF document. The printer page it treated as if it was a big graphics area that you can draw text, shapes, polygons, stamps, lines, and points using the same graphics statements that you have used in previous chapters.

Turning Printing On and Off

To start printing, all you need to do is turn the printer on with the **print on** statement. Once you are finished creating your page or pages to print execute the **print off** statement.

```
1    # c13_printpage.kbs
2    # print a page with text
3
4    printer on
5
6    x = 100 # start first line 100 pixes down on page
7
8    font "Times New Roman", 30, 100
9    for t = 1 to 10
10       text 0, x, "The number t is " + t
11       x = x + textheight()
12   next t
13
14   printer off
```

Program 83: Printing a Page with Text

```
The number t is 1
The number t is 2
The number t is 3
The number t is 4
The number t is 5
The number t is 6
The number t is 7
The number t is 8
The number t is 9
The number t is 10
```

Sample Output 83: Printing a Page with Text

printer on
printeron

Turn printing on. Once printing is turned on the graphic statements (**line**, **plot**, **text**, **rect**, **circle**, **poly**, **stamp**, **graphwidth**, **graphheight**, **textwidth**, and **textheight**) now draw on and return information about the printer page.

New Concept

```
printer off
printeroff
```

Ends the current print document. If your output is being send to a print device the document will start printing. If you output is going to a PDF file the file will be written to the specified location.

New Concept

```
textwidth( string )
textheight()
```

Returns the width or height of a string in pixels when it is draw on the graphics or printer output area with the **text** statement.

The actual width of the string is returned by **textwidth** but **textheight** returns the standard height in pixels of the currently active font.

You may change the printing destination and properties about the page by selecting "Printing" tab on the "Preferences" window. You may select any configured printer, the size of the page, and the orientation of the page.

Additionally you may select the printer page resolution. Screen resolution, the default, draws on the printer page in a similar manner to how the computer screen is drawn on. In this resolution there are approximately 96 pixels per inch (0.26mm/pixel) . In the High resolution mode you are drawing on the printer page in the printer's native resolution. For most printers and for PDF output that resolution is 1,200 pixels per inch (.021mm/pixel).

Remember that the **font** statement uses the unit of "point" to measure the size of text that is drawn to the graphics display. A point is 1/72 of an inch (3.5mm) so the text will remain constant regardless of the printer mode specified.

All of the examples in this chapter are formatted for Letter (8 ½ x 11 inch)
paper in Screen resolution.

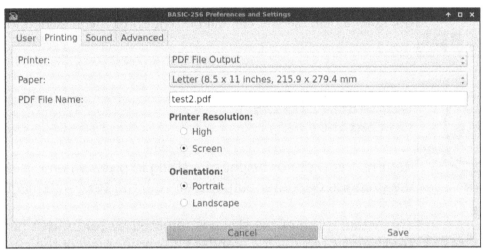

Illustration 23: Preferences – Printing Tab

```
1     # c13_drawpage.kbs
2     # Draw on the page
3
4     printer on
5
6     # put the text in the CENTER of the page
7     color black
8     font "Arial", 40, 500
9     words$ = "Center"
10    x = ( graphwidth - textwidth(words$) ) / 2
11    y = ( graphheight - textheight() ) / 2
12    text x,y,words$
13
14    # draw a circle around the text
15    # fill with clear
16    color black, clear
```

```
17    penwidth 5
18    circle graphwidth/2, graphheight/2, 100
19
20    # draw a triangle using poly
21    color black, grey
22    penwidth 10
23    poly {200,100, 300,300, 100,300 }
24
25
26    # draw a morier pattern on the page
27    color black
28    penwidth 1
29    for t = 0 to 400 step 3
30       line graphwidth, graphheight, graphwidth-400,
      graphheight-t
31       line graphwidth, graphheight, graphwidth-t,
      graphheight-400
32    next t
33
34    printer off
```

Program 84: Printing a Page with Graphics

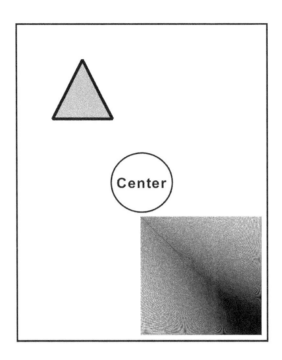

Sample Output 84: Printing a Page with Graphics

New Concept

```
printer page
printerpage
```

if you need to print to a new page just execute the **printer page** statement. This will save the current page and all new output will go into the next page.

```
printer cancel
printercancel
```

If you have started to print a document but decide you do not want to finish it, the **printer cancel** statement will turn off printing and not output the document.

New Concept

The "Big Program" for this chapter uses the printer statements to generate and print a multiplication table.

Big Program

```
1      # c13_multtable.kbs
2      # print a 12x12 multiplication table
3
4      printer on
5      color black
6      font "Arial", 12, 100
7
8      # size of a cell on grid
9      w = 700/13
10     h = textheight()*2
11     #
12     pad = 5
13
14     # draw the grid
15     penwidth 2
16     for x = 0 to 14
17         line x*w,0,x*w,14*h
```

```
18    next x
19    for y = 0 to 14
20       line 0,y*h,14*w,y*h
21    next y
22
23    # put the row and column header numbers
24    font "Arial", 12, 100
25    for x = 0 to 12
26       text (x+1)*w+pad,pad,x
27    next x
28    for y = 0 to 12
29       text pad,(y+1)*h+pad,y
30    next y
31
32    # put the products
33    font "Arial", 12, 50
34    for x = 0 to 12
35       for y = 0 to 12
36          text (x+1)*w+pad,(y+1)*h+pad,(x*y)
37       next y
38    next x
39
40    printer off
```

Program 85: Multiplication Table

	0	1	2	3	4	5	6	7	8	9	10	11	12
0	0	0	0	0	0	0	0	0	0	0	0	0	0
1	0	1	2	3	4	5	6	7	8	9	10	11	12
2	0	2	4	6	8	10	12	14	16	18	20	22	24
3	0	3	6	9	12	15	18	21	24	27	30	33	36
4	0	4	8	12	16	20	24	28	32	36	40	44	48
5	0	5	10	15	20	25	30	35	40	45	50	55	60
6	0	6	12	18	24	30	36	42	48	54	60	66	72
7	0	7	14	21	28	35	42	49	56	63	70	77	84
8	0	8	16	24	32	40	48	56	64	72	80	88	96
9	0	9	18	27	36	45	54	63	72	81	90	99	108
10	0	10	20	30	40	50	60	70	80	90	100	110	120
11	0	11	22	33	44	55	66	77	88	99	110	121	132
12	0	12	24	36	48	60	72	84	96	108	120	132	144

Sample Output 85: Multiplication Table

Exercises:

Word Search

```
k l a n d s c a p e
j f d r e p a p t g
p o r t r a i t x a
b s g n i t t e s p
t h g i e h t x e t
r e s o l u t i o n
o k p r i n t e r o
m a r g i n d f d p
g h t d i w t x e t
o z c a n c e l x p
```

cancel, landscape, margin, page, paper, pdf, portrait, printer, resolution, settings, textheight, textwidth

Problems

13.1. Take your program from Problem 5.1 or 5.2 and have it print the song lyrics on a page after the user types in words to fill in the blanks.

You may need to keep a variable with the line number you are outputting so that you can calculate how far down the page each to start the line.

13.2. Use the smiling face subroutine you created for Problem 9.1 to create a page with a smiling face in the four corners and "Smile!" centered on the page.

Chapter 14: Arrays – Collections of Information.

We have used simple string and numeric variables in many programs, but they can only contain one value at a time. Often we need to work with collections or lists of values. We can do this with either one-dimensioned or two-dimensioned arrays. This chapter will show you how to create, initialize, use, and re-size arrays.

One-Dimensional Arrays of Numbers:

A one-dimensional array allows us to create a list in memory and to access the items in that list by a numeric address (called an index). Arrays can be either numeric or string depending on the type of variable used in the *dim* statement.

```
1    # c14_arraynumeric1d.kbs
2    # one-dimensional numeric array
3
4    dim a(10)
5
6    a[0] = 100
7    a[1] = 200
8    a[3] = a[1] + a[2]
9
10   input "Enter a number> ", a[9]
11   a[8] = a[9] - a[3]
12
13   for t = 0 to 9
14       print "a[" + t + "] = " + a[t]
15   next t
```

Program 86: One-dimensional Numeric Array

```
Enter a number> 63
a[0] = 100
a[1] = 200
a[2] = 0
a[3] = 200
a[4] = 0
a[5] = 0
a[6] = 0
a[7] = 0
a[8] = -137
a[9] = 63
```

Sample Output 86: One-dimensional Numeric Array

New Concept

```
dim variable(items)
dim variable$(items)
dim variable(rows, columns)
dim variable$(rows, columns)
```

The **dim** statement creates an array in the computer's memory the size that was specified in the parenthesis. Sizes (items, rows, and columns) must be integer values greater than or equal to one (1).

The **dim** statement will initialize the elements in the new array with either zero (0) if numeric or the empty string (""), depending on the type of variable.

New Concept

```
variable[index]
variable[rowindex, columnindex]
variable$[index]
variable$[rowindex, columnindex]
```

You can use an array reference (variable with index(s) in square brackets) in your program almost anywhere you can use a simple variable. The index or indexes must be integer values between zero (0) and one less than the size used in the *dim* statement.

It may be confusing, but BASIC-256 uses zero (0) for the first element in an array and the last element has an index one less than the size. Computer people call this a zero-indexed array.

We can use arrays of numbers to draw many balls bouncing on the screen at once. Program 86 uses 5 arrays to store the location of each of the balls, it's direction, and color. Loops are then used to initialize the arrays and to animate the balls. This program also uses the *rgb()* function to calculate and save the color values for each of the balls.

```
1    # c14_manyballbounce.kbs
2    # use arrays to keep up with the direction,
3    # location, and color of many balls on the screen
4
5    fastgraphics
6
7    r = 10  # size of ball
8    balls = 50  # number of balls
9
10   dim x(balls)
11   dim y(balls)
12   dim dx(balls)
13   dim dy(balls)
14   dim colors(balls)
15
```

```
16    for b = 0 to balls-1
17       # starting position of balls
18       x[b] = 0
19       y[b] = 0
20       # speed in x and y directions
21       dx[b] = rand * r + 2
22       dy[b] = rand * r + 2
23       # each ball has it's own color
24       colors[b] = rgb(rand*256, rand*256, rand*256)
25    next b
26
27    color green
28    rect 0,0,300,300
29
30    while true
31       # erase screen
32       clg
33       # now position and draw the balls
34       for b = 0 to balls -1
35          x[b] = x[b] + dx[b]
36          y[b] = y[b] + dy[b]
37          # if off the edges turn the ball around
38          if x[b] < 0 or x[b] > 300 then
39             dx[b] = dx[b] * -1
40          end if
41          # if off the top of bottom turn the ball around
42          if y[b] < 0 or y[b] > 300 then
43             dy[b] = dy[b] * -1
44          end if
45          # draw new ball
46          color colors[b]
47          circle x[b],y[b],r
48       next b
49       # update the display
50       refresh
51       pause .05
52    end while
```

Program 87: Bounce Many Balls

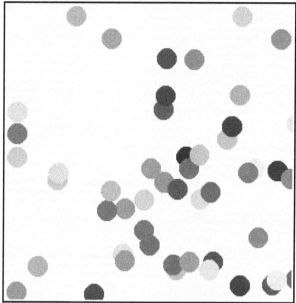

Sample Output 87: Bounce Many Balls

Another example of a ball bouncing can be seen in Program 88. This second example uses sprites and two arrays to keep track of the direction each sprite is moving.

```
1      # c14_manyballsprite.kbs
2      # another way to bounce many balls using sprites
3
4      fastgraphics
5      color white
6      rect 0, 0, graphwidth, graphheight
7
8      n = 20
9      spritedim n
10
11     dim dx(n)
```

```
12      dim dy(n)
13
14      for b = 0 to n-1
15          spriteload b, "greenball.png"
16          spriteplace b,graphwidth/2,graphheight/2
17          spriteshow b
18          dx[b] = rand * 5 + 2
19          dy[b] = rand * 5 + 2
20      next b
21
22      while true
23          for b = 0 to n-1
24              if spritex(b) <=0 or spritex(b) >= graphwidth
        -1 then
25                  dx[b] = dx[b] * -1
26              end if
27              if spritey(b) <= 0 or spritey(b) >= graphheight
        -1 then
28                  dy[b] = dy[b] * -1
29              end if
30              spritemove b, dx[b], dy[b]
31          next b
32          refresh
33      end while
```

Program 88: Bounce Many Balls Using Sprites

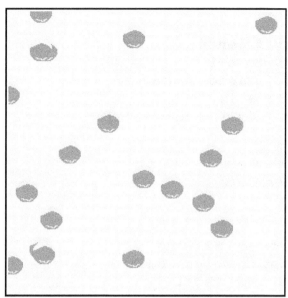

Sample Output 88: Bounce Many Balls Using Sprites

Arrays of Strings:

Arrays can also be used to store string values. To create a string array use a string variable in the *dim* statement. All of the rules about numeric arrays apply to a string array except the data type is different. You can see the use of a string array in Program 89.

```
1     # c14_listoffriends.kbs
2     # use a string array to store names
3
4     print "make a list of my friends"
5     input "how many friends do you have?", n
6
7     dim names$(n)
8
9     for i = 0 to n-1
10        input "enter friend name ?", names$[i]
11    next i
```

```
12
13    cls
14    print "my friends"
15    for i = 0 to n-1
16        print "friend number ";
17        print i + 1;
18        print " is " + names$[i]
19    next i
20    end
```

Program 89: List of My Friends

```
make a list of my friends
how many friends do you have?3
enter friend name ?Bill
enter friend name ?Ken
enter friend name ?Sam
 - screen clears -
my friends
friend number 1 is Bill
friend number 2 is Ken
friend number 3 is Sam
```

Sample Output 89: List of My Friends

Assigning Arrays:

We have seen the use of the curly brackets ({}) to play music, draw polygons, and define stamps. The curly brackets can also be used to create and assign an entire array with custom values.

```
1     # c14_arrayassign.kbs
2     # using a list of values to create an assign an array
3
4     number = {56, 99, 145}
```

```
5      name$ = {"Bob", "Jim", "Susan"}
6
7      for i = 0 to 2
8         print number[i] + " " + name$[i]
9      next i
```

Program 90: Assigning an Array With a List

```
56 Bob
99 Jim
145 Susan
```

Sample Output 90: Assigning an Array With a List

	`array = {value0, value1, … }`
	`array$ = {value0, value1, … }`
	
	A variable will be dimensioned into an array and assigned values (starting with index 0) from a list enclosed in curly braces. This works for numeric and string arrays.

New Concept

Sound and Arrays:

In Chapter 3 we saw how to use a list of frequencies and durations (enclosed in curly braces) to play multiple sounds at once. The sound statement will also accept a list of frequencies and durations from an array. The array should have an even number of elements; the frequencies should be stored in element 0, 2, 4, …; and the durations should be in elements 1, 3, 5, ….

The sample (Program 91) below uses a simple linear formula to make a fun sonic chirp.

```
1      # c14_spacechirp.kbs
2      # play a spacy sound
3
4      # even values 0,2,4... - frequency
5      # odd values 1,3,5... - duration
6
7      # chirp starts at 100hz and increases by 40 for each
       of the 50 total sounds in list, duration is always 10
8
9      dim a(100)
10     for i = 0 to 98 step 2
11        a[i] = i * 40 + 100
12        a[i+1] = 10
13     next i
14     sound a
15     end
```

Program 91: Space Chirp Sound

 **Explore** What kind of crazy sounds can you program. Experiment with the formulas you use to change the frequencies and durations.

Graphics and Arrays:

In Chapter 8 we also saw the use of lists for creating polygons and stamps. Arrays may also be used to draw stamps, polygons, and sprites. This may help simplify your code by allowing the same shape to be defined once, stored in an array, and used in various places in your program.

In an array used for a shape, the even elements (0, 2, 4, ...) contain the x value for each of the points and the odd element (1, 3, 5, ...) contain the y value for the points. The array will have two values for each point in the shape.

In Program 92 we will use the stamp from the mouse chapter to draw a big X with a shadow. This is accomplished by stamping a gray shape shifted in the direction of the desired shadow and then stamping the object that is projecting the shadow.

```
1     # c14_shadowstamp.kbs
2     # create a stamp from an array
3
4     xmark = {-1, -2, 0, -1, 1, -2, 2, -1, 1, 0, 2, 1, 1,
      2, 0, 1, -1, 2, -2, 1, -1, 0, -2, -1}
5
6     clg
7     color grey
8     stamp 160,165,50,xmark
9     color black
10    stamp 150,150,50,xmark
```

Program 92: Shadow Stamp

Sample Output 92: Shadow Stamp

Arrays can also be used to create stamps or polygons mathematically. In Program 93 we create an array with 10 elements (5 points) and assign random locations to each of the points to draw random polygons. BASIC-256 will fill the shape the best it can but when lines cross, as you will see, the fill sometimes leaves gaps and holes.

```
1      # c14_randompoly.kbs
2      # make an 5 sided random polygon
3
4      dim shape(10)
5
6      for t = 0 to 8 step 2
7         x = 300 * rand
8         y = 300 * rand
9         shape[t] = x
10        shape[t+1] = y
11     next t
12
```

```
13    clg
14    color black
15    poly shape
```
Program 93: Randomly Create a Polygon

Sample Output 93: Randomly Create a Polygon

Advanced - Two Dimensional Arrays:

So far in this chapter we have explored arrays as lists of numbers or strings. We call these simple arrays one-dimensional arrays because they resemble a line of values. Arrays may also be created with two-dimensions representing rows and columns of data. Program 94 uses both one and two-dimensional arrays to calculate student's average grade.

```
1    # c14_grades.kbs
2    # calculate average grades for each student
```

```
3       # and whole class using a two dimensional array
4
5       nstudents = 3 # number of students
6       nscores = 4 # number of scores per student
7
8       dim students$(nstudents)
9       dim grades(nstudents, nscores)
10
11      # store the scores as columns and the students as
        rows
12      # first student
13      students$[0] = "Jim"
14      grades[0,0] = 90
15      grades[0,1] = 92
16      grades[0,2] = 81
17      grades[0,3] = 55
18      # second student
19      students$[1] = "Sue"
20      grades[1,0] = 66
21      grades[1,1] = 99
22      grades[1,2] = 98
23      grades[1,3] = 88
24      # third student
25      students$[2] = "Tony"
26      grades[2,0] = 79
27      grades[2,1] = 81
28      grades[2,2] = 87
29      grades[2,3] = 73
30
31      total = 0
32      for row = 0 to nstudents-1
33         studenttotal = 0
34         for column = 0 to nscores-1
35            studenttotal = studenttotal + grades[row,
        column]
36            total = total + grades[row, column]
37         next column
38         print students$[row] + "'s average is ";
39         print studenttotal / nscores
```

```
40    next row
41    print "class average is ";
42    print total / (nscores * nstudents)
43
44    end
```

Program 94: Grade Calculator

```
Jim's average is 79.5
Sue's average is 87.75
Tony's average is 80
class average is 82.416667
```

Sample Output 94: Grade Calculator

Really Advanced - Array Sizes and Passing Arrays to Subroutines and Functions:

Sometimes we need to create programming code that would work with an array of any size. If you specify a question mark as a index, row, or column number in the square bracket reference of an array BASIC-256 will return the dimensioned size. In Program 90 we modified Program 87 to display the array regardless of it's length. You will see the special [?] used on line 16 to return the current size of the array.

```
1    # c14_size.kbs
2    # arraylength and passing to subroutine
3
4    print "The Number Array:"
5    number = {77, 55, 33}
6    call showarray(ref(number))
7
8    print "The Random Array:"
9    dim r(5)
```

```
10      for a = 0 to r[?] - 1
11          r[a] = int(rand*10)+1
12      next a
13      call showarray(ref(r))
14      #
15      end
16      #
17      subroutine showarray(ref(a))
18          print "has " + a[?] + " elements."
19          for i = 0 to a[?] - 1
20              print "element " + i + " " + a[i]
21          next i
22      end subroutine
```

Program 95: Get Array Size

```
The Number Array:
has 3 elements.
element 0 77
element 1 55
element 2 33
The Random Array:
has 5 elements.
element 0 7
element 1 5
element 2 1
element 3 9
element 4 10
```

Sample Output 95: Get Array Size

```
array[?]
array$[?]
array[?,]
array$[?,]
array[,?]
array$[,?]
```

New Concept

The [?] returns the length of a one-dimensional array or the total number of elements (rows * column) in a two-dimensional array. The [?,] reference returns the number of rows and the [,?] reference returns the number of columns of a two dimensional array.

```
ref(array)
ref(array$)
```

The ref() function is used to pass a reference to an array to a function or subroutine. The array reference must be specified in the subroutine/function creation and when it is called.

New Concept

If the subroutine changes an element in the referenced array the value in the array will change outside the subroutine or function. Remember this is different behavior than other variables, whos values are copied to new variables within the function or subroutine.

Really Really Advanced - Resizing Arrays:

BASIC-256 will also allow you to re-dimension an existing array. The *redim* statement will allow you to re-size an array and will preserve the existing data. If the new array is larger, the new elements will be filled with zero (0) or the empty string (""). If the new array is smaller, the values beyond the new size will be truncated (cut off).

```
1     # c14_redim.kbs
2
3     number = {77, 55, 33}
4     # create a new element on the end
5     redim number(4)
6     number[3] = 22
7     #
8     for i = 0 to 3
9         print i + " " + number[i]
10    next i
```

Program 96: Re-Dimension an Array

```
0 77
1 55
2 33
3 22
```

Sample Output 96: Re-Dimension an Array

New Concept

```
redim variable(items)
redim variable$(items)
redim variable(rows, columns)
redim variable$(rows, columns)
```

The **redim** statement re-sizes an array in the computer's memory. Data previously stored in the array will be kept, if it fits.

When resizing two-dimensional arrays the values are copied in a linear manner. Data may be shifted in an unwanted manner if you are changing the number of columns.

Big Program

The "Big Program" for this chapter uses three numeric arrays to store the positions and speed of falling space debris. You are not playing pong but you are trying to avoid all of them to score points.

```
1     # c14_spacewarp.kbs
2     # the falling space debris game
3
4     # setup balls and arrays for them
5     balln = 5
6     dim ballx(balln)
7     dim bally(balln)
8     dim ballspeed(balln)
9     ballr = 10      # radius of balls
10
11    # setup minimum and maximum values
12    minx = ballr
13    maxx = graphwidth - ballr
14    miny = ballr
15    maxy = graphheight - ballr
16
17    # initial score
18    score = 0
19
20    # setup player size, move distance, and location
21    playerw = 30
22    playerm = 10
23    playerh = 10
24    playerx = (graphwidth - playerw)/2
25
26    # setup other variables
27    keyj = asc("J")      # value for the 'j' key
28    keyk = asc("K")      # value for the 'k' key
```

```
29    keyq = asc("Q")      # value for the 'q' key
30    growpercent = .20   # random growth - bigger is faster
31    speed = .15    # the lower the faster
32
33    print "spacewarp - use j and k keys to avoid the
      falling space debris"
34    print "q to quit"
35
36    fastgraphics
37
38    # setup initial ball positions and speed
39    for n = 0 to balln-1
40       bally[n] = miny
41       ballx[n] = int(rand * (maxx-minx)) + minx
42       ballspeed[n] = int(rand * (2*ballr)) + 1
43    next n
44
45    more = true
46    while more
47       pause speed
48       score = score + 1
49
50       # clear screen
51       color black
52       rect 0, 0, graphwidth, graphheight
53
54       # draw balls and check for collission
55       color white
56       for n = 0 to balln-1
57          bally[n] = bally[n] + ballspeed[n]
58          if bally[n] > maxy then
59             # ball fell off of bottom - put back at top
60             bally[n] = miny
61             ballx[n] = int(rand * (maxx-minx)) + minx
62             ballspeed[n] = int(rand * (2*ballr)) + 1
63          end if
64          circle ballx[n], bally[n], ballr
```

```
65              if ((bally[n]) >= (maxy-playerh-ballr)) and
        ((ballx[n]+ballr) >= playerx) and ((ballx[n]-ballr)
        <= (playerx+playerw)) then more = false
66       next n
67
68       # draw player
69       color red
70       rect playerx, maxy - playerh, playerw, playerh
71       refresh
72
73       # make player bigger
74       if (rand<growpercent) then playerw = playerw + 1
75
76       # get player key and move if key pressed
77       k = key
78       if k = keyj then playerx = playerx - playerm
79       if k = keyk then playerx = playerx + playerm
80       if k = keyq then more = false
81
82       # keep player on screen
83       if playerx < 0 then playerx = 0
84       if playerx > graphwidth - playerw then playerx =
        graphwidth - playerw
85
86     end while
87
88     print "score " + string(score)
89     print "you died."
90     end
```

Program 97: Big Program - Space Warp Game

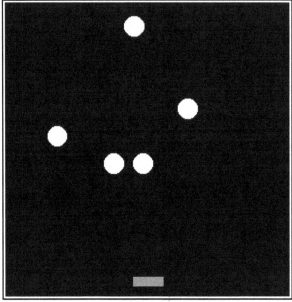

Sample Output 97: Big Program - Space Warp Game

Exercises:

Word Search

```
a t d v i t f p a u
y o y n s z o n c b
e r d q a i m n o e
o e o s c o l u m n
x e d m c z d y v i
c o l l e c t i o n
a r r a y m n h z y
y h t s i l e g d f
d i m e n s i o n l
y j n f z r o w l t
```

array, collection, column, dimension, index, list, memory, row

Problems

14.1. Ask the user for how many numbers they want to add together and display the total. Create an array of the user chosen size, prompt the user to enter the numbers and store them in the array. Once the numbers are entered loop through the array elements and print the total of them.

14.2. Add to Problem 14.1 logic to display the average after calculating the total.

14.3. Add to Problem 14.1 logic to display the minimum and the maximum values. To calculate the minimum: 1) copy the first element in the array into a variable; 2) compare all of the remaining elements to the variable and if it is less than the saved value then save the new minimum.

14.4. Take the program from Problem 14.2 and 14.3 and create functions to calculate and return the minimum, maximum, and average. Pass the array to the function and use the array length operator to make the functions work with any array passed.

14.5. Create a program that asks for a sequence of numbers, like in Problem 14.1. Once the user has entered the numbers to the array display a table of each number multiplied by each other number. Hint: you will need a loop nested inside another loop.

```
n> 5
number 0> 4
number 1> 7
number 2> 9
number 3> 12
number 4> 45
16 28 36 48 180
28 49 63 84 315
36 63 81 108 405
48 84 108 144 540
180 315 405 540 2025
```

Chapter 15: Mathematics – More Fun With Numbers.

In this chapter we will look at some additional mathematical operators and functions that work with numbers. Topics will be broken down into four sections: 1) new operators; 2) new integer functions, 3) new floating point functions, and 4) trigonometric functions.

New Operators:

In addition to the basic mathematical operations we have been using since the first chapter, there are three more operators in BASIC-256. Operations similar to these three operations exist in most computer languages. They are the operations of modulo, integer division, and power.

Operation	Operator	Description
Modulo	%	Return the remainder of an integer division.
Integer Division	\	Return the whole number of times one integer can be divided into another.
Power	^	Raise a number to the power of another number.

Modulo Operator:

The modulo operation returns the remainder part of integer division. When you do long division with whole numbers, you get a remainder – that is the same as the modulo.

```
1       # c15_modulo.kbs
```

```
2        input "enter a number ", n
3        if n % 2 = 0 then print "divisible by 2"
4        if n % 3 = 0 then print "divisible by 3"
5        if n % 5 = 0 then print "divisible by 5"
6        if n % 7 = 0 then print "divisible by 7"
7        end
```

Program 98: The Modulo Operator

```
enter a number 10
divisible by 2
divisible by 5
```

Sample Output 98: The Modulo Operator

New Concept	***expression1 % expression2*** The Modulo (%) operator performs integer division of *expression1* divided by *expression2* and returns the remainder of that process. If one or both of the expressions are not integer values (whole numbers) they will be converted to an integer value by truncating the decimal (like in the *int()* function) portion before the operation is performed.

You might not think it, but the modulo operator (%) is used quite often by programmers. Two common uses are; 1) to test if one number divides into another (Program 98) and 2) to limit a number to a specific range (Program 99).

```
1        # c15_moveballmod.kbs
```

```
2     # rewrite of moveball.kbs using the modulo operator
      to wrap the ball around the screen
3
4     print "use i for up, j for left, k for right, m for
      down, q to quit"
5
6     fastgraphics
7     clg
8     ballradius = 20
9
10    # position of the ball
11    # start in the center of the screen
12    x = graphwidth /2
13    y = graphheight / 2
14
15    # draw the ball initially on the screen
16    call drawball(x, y, ballradius)
17
18    # loop and wait for the user to press a key
19    while true
20       k = key
21       if k = asc("I") then
22          # y can go negative, + graphheight keeps it
      positive
23          y = (y - ballradius + graphheight) %
      graphheight
24          call drawball(x, y, ballradius)
25       end if
26       if k = asc("J") then
27          x = (x - ballradius + graphwidth) % graphwidth
28          call drawball(x, y, ballradius)
29       end if
30       if k = asc("K") then
31          x = (x + ballradius) % graphwidth
32          call drawball(x, y, ballradius)
33       end if
34       if k = asc("M") then
35          y = (y + ballradius) % graphheight
36          call drawball(x, y, ballradius)
```

```
37          end if
38          if k = asc("Q") then end
39      end while
40
41      subroutine drawball(bx, by, br)
42          color white
43          rect 0, 0, graphwidth, graphheight
44          color red
45          circle bx, by, br
46          refresh
47      end subroutine
```

Program 99: Move Ball - Use Modulo to Keep on Screen

Integer Division Operator:

The Integer Division (\) operator does normal division but it works only with integers (whole numbers) and returns an integer value. As an example, 13 divided by 4 is 3 remainder 1 – so the result of the integer division is 3.

```
1       # c15_integerdivision.kbs
2       input "dividend ", dividend
3       input "divisor ", divisor
4       print dividend + " / " + divisor + " is ";
5       print dividend \ divisor;
6       print "r";
7       print dividend % divisor;
```

Program 100: Check Your Long Division

```
dividend 43
divisor 6
43 / 6 is 7r1
```

Sample Output 100: Check Your Long Division

New Concept

expression1 \ expression2

The Integer Division (\) operator performs division of *expression1 / expression2* and returns the whole number of times *expression1* goes into *expression2*.

If one or both of the expressions are not integer values (whole numbers), they will be converted to an integer value by truncating the decimal (like in the *int()* function) portion before the operation is performed.

Power Operator:

The power operator will raise one number to the power of another number.

```
1    # c15_power.kbs
2    for t = 0 to 16
3        print "2 ^ " + t + " = ";
4        print 2 ^ t
5    next t
```

Program 101: The Powers of Two

```
2 ^ 0 = 1
2 ^ 1 = 2
2 ^ 2 = 4
2 ^ 3 = 8
2 ^ 4 = 16
2 ^ 5 = 32
2 ^ 6 = 64
2 ^ 7 = 128
2 ^ 8 = 256
2 ^ 9 = 512
2 ^ 10 = 1024
```

```
2 ^ 11 = 2048
2 ^ 12 = 4096
2 ^ 13 = 8192
2 ^ 14 = 16384
2 ^ 15 = 32768
2 ^ 16 = 65536
```

Sample Output 101: The Powers of Two

expression1 ^ expression2

The Power (^) operator raises *expression1* to the *expression2* power.

The mathematical expression $a=b^c$ would be written in BASIC-256 as a = b ^ c.

New Integer Functions:

The three new integer functions in this chapter all deal with how to convert strings and floating point numbers to integer values. All three functions handle the decimal part of the conversion differently.

In the *int()* function the decimal part is just thrown away, this has the same effect of subtracting the decimal part from positive numbers and adding it to negative numbers. This can cause troubles if we are trying to round and there are numbers less than zero (0).

The *ceil()* and *floor()* functions sort of fix the problem with *int()*. Ceil() always adds enough to every floating point number to bring it up to the next whole number while floor(0) always subtracts enough to bring the floating point number down to the closest integer.

We have been taught to round a number by simply adding 0.5 and drop the decimal part. If we use the int() function, it will work for positive numbers but not for negative numbers. In BASIC-256 to round we should always use a formula like $a = floor(b+0.5)$.

	Function	Description
New Concept	int(*expression*)	Convert an expression (string, integer, or decimal value) to an integer (whole number). When converting a floating point value the decimal part is truncated (ignored). If a string does not contain a number a zero is returned.
	ceil(*expression*)	Converts a floating point value to the next highest integer value.
	floor(*expression*)	Converts a floating point expression to the next lowers integer value. You should use this function for rounding $a = floor(b+0.5)$.

```
1    # c15_intceilfloor.kbs
2    for t = 1 to 10
3        n = rand * 100 - 50
4        print n;
5        print "  int=" + int(n);
6        print "  ceil=" + ceil(n);
7        print "  floor=" + floor(n)
8    next t
```

Program 102: Difference Between Int, Ceiling, and Floor

```
-46.850173  int=-46  ceil=-46  floor=-47
```

```
-43.071987  int=-43  ceil=-43  floor=-44
23.380133  int=23  ceil=24  floor=23
4.620722  int=4  ceil=5  floor=4
3.413543  int=3  ceil=4  floor=3
-26.608505  int=-26  ceil=-26  floor=-27
-18.813465  int=-18  ceil=-18  floor=-19
7.096065  int=7  ceil=8  floor=7
23.482759  int=23  ceil=24  floor=23
-45.463169  int=-45  ceil=-45  floor=-46
```

Sample Output 102: Difference Between Int, Ceiling, and Floor

New Floating Point Functions:

The mathematical functions that wrap up this chapter are ones you may need to use to write some programs. In the vast majority of programs these functions will not be needed.

	Function	Description
New Concept	`float(expression)`	Convert expression (string, integer, or decimal value) to a decimal value. Useful in changing strings to numbers. If a string does not contain a number a zero is returned.
	`abs(expression)`	Converts a floating point or integer expression to an absolute value.
	`log(expression)`	Returns the natural logarithm (base *e*) of a number.
	`log10(expression)`	Returns the base 10 logarithm of a number.

Advanced - Trigonometric Functions:

Trigonometry is the study of angles and measurement. BASIC-256 includes support for the common trigonometric functions. Angular measure is done in radians (0-2p). If you are using degrees (0-360) in your programs you must convert to use the "trig" functions.

	Function	Description
New Concept	cos (*expression*)	Return the cosine of an angle.
	sin (*expression*)	Return the sine of an angle.
	tan (*expression*)	Return the tangent of an angle.
	degrees (*expression*)	Convert Radians $(0 - 2\pi)$ to Degrees (0-360).
	radians (*expression*)	Convert Degrees (0-360) to Radians $(0 - 2\pi)$.
	acos (*expression*)	Return the inverse cosine.
	asin (*expression*)	Return the inverse sine.
	atan (*expression*)	Return the inverse tangent.

The discussion of the first three functions will refer to the sides of a right triangle. Illustration 24 shows one of these with it's sides and angles labeled.

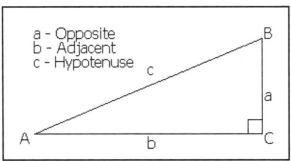

Illustration 24: Right Triangle

Cosine:

A cosine is the ratio of the length of the adjacent leg over the length of the hypotenuse $\cos A = \frac{b}{c}$. The cosine repeats itself every 2π radians and has a range from -1 to 1. Illustration 24 graphs a cosine wave from 0 to 2π radians.

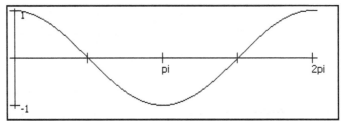

Illustration 25: Cos() Function

Sine:

The sine is the ratio of the opposite leg over the hypotenuse $\sin A = \frac{a}{c}$.

The sine repeats itself every 2π radians and has a range from -1 to 1. You have seen diagrams of sine waves in Chapter 3 as music was discussed.

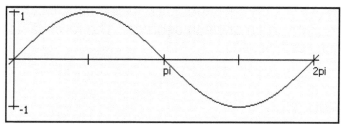

Illustration 26: Sin() Function

Tangent:

The tangent is the ratio of the adjacent side over the opposite side

$\tan A = \dfrac{a}{b}$. The tangent repeats itself every π radians and has a range from

-∞ to ∞. The tangent has this range because when the angle approaches ½π radians the opposite side gets very small and will actually be zero when the angle is ½π radians.

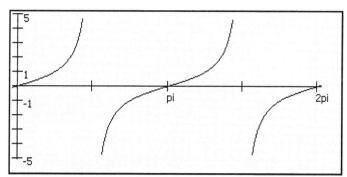

Illustration 27: Tan() Function

Degrees Function:

The **degrees**() function does the quick mathematical calculation to convert an angle in radians to an angle in degrees. The formula used is
$degrees = radians / 2\pi * 360$.

Radians Function:

The **radians**() function will convert degrees to radians using the formula
$radians = degrees / 360 * 2\pi$. Remember all of the trigonometric functions in BASIC-256 use radians and not degrees to measure angles.

Inverse Cosine:

The inverse cosine function **acos**() will return an angle measurement in radians for the specified cosine value. This function performs the opposite of the *cos()* function.

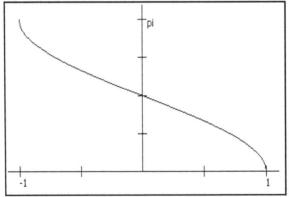

Illustration 28: Acos() Function

Inverse Sine:

The inverse sine function **asin**() will return an angle measurement in radians for the specified sine value. This function performs the opposite of the sin*()* function.

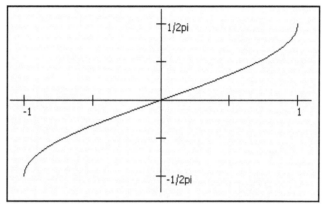

Illustration 29: Asin() Function

Inverse Tangent:

The inverse tangent function **atan**() will return an angle measurement in radians for the specified tangent value. This function performs the opposite of the **tan**() function.

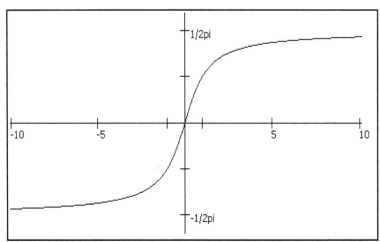

Illustration 30: Atan() Function

 The big program this chapter allows the user to enter two positive whole numbers and then performs long division. This program used logarithms to calculate how long the numbers are, modulo and integer division to get the individual digits, and is generally a very complex program. Don't be scared or put off if you don't understand exactly how it works, yet.

Big Program

```
1     # c15_handyclock.kbs
2
3     fastgraphics
4
```

```
5    while true
6       clg
7       # draw outline
8       color black, white
9       penwidth 5
10      circle 150,150,105
11      # draw the 60 marks (every fifth one make it
     larger)
12      color black
13      penwidth 1
14      for m = 0 to 59
15         a = 2 * pi * m / 60
16         if m % 5 = 0 then
17            pip = 5
18         else
19            pip = 1
20         end if
21         circle 150-sin(a)*95,150-cos(a)*95,pip
22      next m
23      # draw the hands
24      h = hour % 12 * 60 / 12 + minute/12 + second /
     3600
25      call drawhand(150,150,h,50,6,green)
26      m = minute + second / 60
27      call drawhand(150,150,m,75,4,red)
28      call drawhand(150,150,second,100,3,blue)
29      refresh
30      pause 1
31   end while
32
33   subroutine drawhand(x, y, f, l, w, handcolor)
34      # pass the location x and y
35      # f as location on face of clock 0-59
36      # length, width, and color of the hand
37      color handcolor
38      stamp x, y, 1, f/60*2*pi - pi / 2, {0,-w,l,0,0,w}
39   end subroutine
```

Program 103: Big Program – Clock with Hands

Sample Output 103: Big Program – Clock with Hands

Exercises:

Word Search

```
e c e i l i n g n d a b
f t z n n u r a r b g s
c y i t a e t e s m o k
f s r s g a m p h c t j
a a r e o a l t a n i s
t o t o i p i l e p d n
t n l n o r p c c o e a
i a d u a l a o o w g i
r e o g d j f s s e r d
r o o l d o i x k r e a
r l p a f n m w c s e r
d s h y p o t e n u s e
```

abs, acos, adjacent, asin, atan, ceiling, cos, degrees, float, floor, hypotenuse, int, integer, logarithm, modulo, opposite, power, radians, remainder, sin, tan

Problems

15.1. Have the user input a decimal number. Display the number it as a whole number and the closest faction over 1000 that is possible.

15.2. Take the program from Problem 15.1 and use a loop to reduce the fraction by dividing the numerator and denominator by common factors.

15.3. Write a program to draw a regular polygon with any number of sides (3 and up). Place it's center in the center of the graphics window and make its vertices 100 pixels from the center. Hint: A circle can be drawn by plotting points a specific radius from a point. The following plots a circle with a radius of 100 pixels around the point 150,150.

```
for a = 0 to 2*pi step .01
    plot 150-100*sin(a),150-100*cos(a)
next a
```

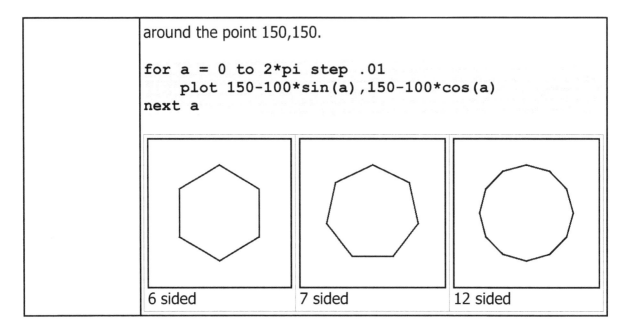

| 6 sided | 7 sided | 12 sided |

Chapter 16: Working with Strings.

We have used strings to store non-numeric information, build output, and capture input. We have also seen, in Chapter 11, using the Unicode values of single characters to build strings.

This chapter shows several new functions that will allow you to manipulate string values.

The String Functions:

BASIC-256 includes eight common functions for the manipulation of strings. Table 8 includes a summary of them.

Function	Description
string(*expression*)	Convert expression (string, integer, or decimal value) to a string value.
length(*string*)	Returns the length of a string.
left(*string, length*)	Returns a string of length characters starting from the left.
right(*string, length*)	Returns a string of length characters starting from the right.
mid(*string, start, length*)	Returns a string of length characters starting from the middle of a string.
upper(*expression*)	Returns an upper case string.
lower(*expression*)	Returns a lower case string.
instr(*haystack, needle*)	Searches the string "haystack" for the "needle" and returns it's location.

Table 8: Summary of String Functions

String() Function:

The **string**() function will take an expression of any format and will return a string. This function is a convenient way to convert an integer or floating point number into characters so that it may be manipulated as a string.

```
1       # c16_string.kbs
2       # convert a number to a string
3
4       a$ = string(10 + 13)
5       print a$
6       b$ = string(2 * pi)
7       print b$
```

Program 104: The String Function

```
23
6.283185
```

Sample Output 104: The String Function

New Concept

string(*expression*)

Convert expression (string, integer, or decimal value) to a string value.

Length() Function:

The *length()* function will take a string expression and return it's length in characters (or letters).

```
1    # c16_length.kbs
2    # find length of a string
3
4    # should print 6, 0, and 17
5    print length("Hello.")
6    print length("")
7    print length("Programming Rulz!")
```

Program 105: The Length Function

```
6
0
17
```

Sample Output 105: The Length Function

New Concept

length(*expression*)

Returns the length of the string expression. Will return zero (0) for the empty string "".

Left(), Right() and Mid() Functions:

The **left**(), **right**(), and **mid**() functions will extract sub-strings (or parts of a string) from a larger string.

```
1     # c16_leftrightmid.kbs
2     # show right, left, and mid string functions
3
4     a$ = "abcdefghijklm"
5
6     print left(a$,4)     # prints first 4 letters
7
8     print right(a$,2)    # prints last 2 letters
9
10    print mid(a$,4,3)    # prints 4th-7th letters
11    print mid(a$,10,9)   # prints 10th and 11th letters
```

Program 106: The Left, Right, and Mid Functions

```
abcd
kl
def
jklm
```

Sample Output 106: The Left, Right, and Mid Functions

New Concept

`left(string, length)`

Return a sub-string from the left end of a string. If length is equal or greater then the actual length of the string the entire string will be returned.

`right(`*`string, length`*`)`

Return a sub-string from the right end of a string. If length is equal or greater then the actual length of the string the entire string will be returned.

`mid(`*`string, start, length`*`)`

Return a sub-string of specified length from somewhere on the middle of a string. The start parameter specifies where the sub-string begins (1 = beginning of string).

Upper() and Lower() Functions:

The **upper**() and **lower**() functions simply will return a string of upper case or lower case letters. These functions are especially helpful when you are trying to perform a comparison of two strings and you do not care what case they actually are.

```
1    # c16_upperlower.kbs
2
3    a$ = "Hello."
4
5    print lower(a$)    # prints all lowercase
6
```

```
7       print upper(a$)    # prints all UPPERCASE
```

Program 107: The Upper and Lower Functions

```
hello.
HELLO.
```

Sample Output 107: The Upper and Lower Functions

New Concept	`lower(`*`string`*`)`
	`upper(`*`string`*`)`
	
	Returns an all upper case or lower case copy of the string expression. Non-alphabetic characters will not be modified.

Instr() Function:

The **instr**() function searches a string for the first occurrence of another string. The return value is the location in the big string of the smaller string. If the substring is not found then the function will return a zero (0).

```
1       # c16_instr.kbs
2       # is one string inside another
3
4       a$ = "abcdefghijklm"
5       print 'the location of "hi" is ';
6       print instr(a$,"hi")
7       print 'the location of "bye" is ';
8       print instr(a$,"bye")
```

Program 108: The Instr Function

```
the location of "hi" is 8
the location of "bye" is 0
```

Sample Output 108: The Instr Function

`instr(haystack, needle)`

Find the sub-string (*needle)* in another string expression (*haystack*). Return the character position of the start. If sub-string is not found return a zero (0).

New Concept

Big Program

The decimal (base 10) numbering system that is most commonly used uses 10 different digits (0-9) to represent numbers.

Imagine if you will what would have happened if there were only 5 digits (0-4) – the number 23 ($2*10^1+3*10^0$) would become 43 ($4*5^1+3*5^0$) to represent the same number of items. This type of transformation is called radix (or base) conversion.

The computer internally does not understand base 10 numbers but converts everything to base 2 (binary) numbers to be stored in memory.

The "Big Program" this chapter will convert a positive integer from any base 2 to 36 (where letters are used for the 11th - 26th digits) to any other base.

```
1    # c16_radix.kbs
2    # convert a number from one base (2-36) to another
3
4    digits$ = "0123456789ABCDEFGHIJKLMNOPQRSTUVWXYZ"
5
6    frombase = getbase("from base")
7    input "number in base " + frombase + " >", number$
8    number$ = upper(number$)
9
10   # convert number to base 10 and store in n
11   n = 0
12   for i = 1 to length(number$)
13      n = n * frombase
14      n = n + instr(digits$, mid(number$, i, 1)) - 1
15   next i
16
17   tobase = getbase("to base")
18
19   # now build string in tobase
20   result$ = ""
21   while n <> 0
22      result$ = mid(digits$, n % tobase + 1, 1) +
     result$
23      n = n \ tobase
24   end while
25
26   print "in base " + tobase + " that number is " +
     result$
27   end
28
29   function getbase(message$)
30      # get a base from 2 to 36
31      do
32         input message$+"> ", base
33      until base >= 2 and base <= 36
34      return base
35   end function
```

Program 109: Big Program - Radix Conversion

```
from base> 10
number in base 10 >999
to base> 16
in base 16 that number is 3E7
```

Sample Output 109: Big Program - Radix Conversion

Exercises:

Word Search

```
u  r  h  t  g  n  e  l
p  g  i  r  a  g  k  f
p  r  n  l  c  f  l  r
e  q  i  i  e  f  e  t
r  d  r  g  r  f  x  s
v  i  i  r  h  t  t  n
p  m  m  x  o  t  s  i
r  e  w  o  l  f  w  i
```

instr, left, length, lower, mid, right, string, upper

Problems

16.1. Have the user enter a string and display the string backwards.

16.2. Modify 16.1 to create a palindrome testing program. Remove all characters from the string that are not letters before reversing it. Compare the results and print a message that the text entered is the same backwards as forwards.

```
enter a string >never odd or even
neveroddoreven
neveroddoreven
is a palindrome
```

16.3. You work for a small retail store that hides the original cost of an item on the price tag using an alphabetic code. The code is "roygbivace" where the letter 'r' is used for a 0, 'o' for a 1, … and 'e' is used for a 9. Write a program that will convert a numeric cost to the code and a code to a cost.

```
cost or code >9.84
```

```
ecb

cost or code >big
4.53
```

16.4: You and your friend want to communicate in a way that your friends can't easily read. The Cesar cipher (http://en.wikipedia.org/wiki/Caesar_cipher) is an easy but not very secure way to encode a message. If you and your friend agree to shift the same number of letters then you can easily share a secret message. Decoding a message is accomplished by applying a shift of 26 minus the original shift.

A sample of some of the shifts for the letters A-D are shown below. Notice that the letters wrap around.

Shift	A	B	C	D
1	B	C	D	E
13	M	N	O	P
25	Z	A	B	C

Write a program that asks for the shift and for a string and displays the text with the cipher applied.

```
shift >4
message >i could really go for
some pizza
M GSYPH VIEPPC KS JSV WSQI TMDDE

shift >22
message >M GSYPH VIEPPC KS JSV
WSQI TMDDE
I COULD REALLY GO FOR SOME PIZZA
```

Chapter 17: Files – Storing Information For Later.

We have explored the computer's short term memory with variables and arrays but how do we store those values for later? There are many different techniques for long term data storage.

BASIC-256 supports writing and reading information from files on your hard disk. That process of input and output is often written as I/O.

This chapter will show you how to read values from a file and then write them for long term storage.

Reading Lines From a File:

Our first program using files is going to show you many of the statements and constants you will need to use to manipulate file data. There are several new statements and functions in this program.

```
1     # c17_read1file.kbs
2     # read a simple text file
3
4     input "file name> ", fn$
5     if not exists(fn$) then
6        print fn$ + " does not exist."
7        end
8     end if
9     #
10    n = 0
11    open fn$
12    while not eof
13       l$ = readline
14       n = n + 1
```

```
15          print n + " " + l$
16      end while
17      #
18      print "the file " + fn$ + " is " + size + " bytes
        long."
19      close
```

Program 110: Read Lines From a File

```
file name> e2_c17_test.txt
1 These are the times that
2 try men's souls.
3 - Thomas Paine
the file e2_c17_test.txt is 57 bytes long.
```

Sample Output 110: Read Lines From a File

exist(*expression*)

Look on the computer for a file name specified by the string *expression*. Drive and path may be specified as part of the file name, but if they are omitted then the current working directory will be the search location.

Returns *true* if the file exists; else returns *false*.

New Concept

```
open expression
open (expression)
open filenumber, expression
open (filenumber, expression)
```

Open the file specified by the *expression* for reading and writing to the specified file number. If the file does not exist it will be created so that information may be added (see *write* and *writeline*). Be sure to execute the *close* statement when the program is finished with the file.

BASIC-256 may have a total of eight (8) files open 0 to 7. If no file number is specified then the file will be opened as file number zero (0).

New Concept

```
eof
eof()
eof(filenumber)
```

The **eof** function returns a value of *true* if we are at the end of the file for reading or *false* if there is still more data to be read.

If filenumber is not specified then file number zero (0) will be used.

New Concept

```
readline
readline()
readline(filenumber)
```

Return a string containing the contents of an open file up to the end of the current line. If we are at the end of the file [*eof(filenumber) = true*] then this function will return the empty string ("").

If filenumber is not specified then file number zero (0) will be used.

New Concept

```
size
size()
size(filenumber)
```

This function returns the length of an open file in bytes.

If filenumber is not specified then file number zero (0) will be used.

New Concept

```
close
close()
close filenumber
close(filenumber)
```

The **close** statement will complete any pending I/O to the file and allow for another file to be opened with the same number.

If filenumber is not specified then file number zero (0) will be used.

Writing Lines to a File:

In Program 110 we saw how to read lines from a file. The next two programs show different variations of how to write information to a file. In Program 111 we open and clear any data that may have been in the file to add our new lines and in Program 112 we append our new lines to the end (saving the previous data).

```
1       # c17_resetwrite.kbs
2       # write text to a file, go back to begining
3       # and display the text
4
5       open "e2_c17_resetwrite.dat"
6
7       print "enter a blank line to close file"
8
9       # clear file (reset) and start over
10      reset
11      while true
12         input ">", l$
13         if l$ = "" then exit while
14         writeline l$
15      end while
16
17      # go the the start and display contents
18      seek 0
19      k = 0
20      while not eof()
21         k = k + 1
22         print k + " " + readline()
23      end while
24
25      close
26      end
```

Program 111: Clear File and Write Lines

```
enter a blank line to close file
>this is some
>data, I am typing
>into the program.
>
1 this is some
2 data, I am typing
3 into the program.
```

Sample Output 111: Clear File and Write Lines

New Concept

```
reset or
reset() or
reset filenumber
reset(filenumber)
```

Clear any data in an open file and move the file pointer to the beginning.

If filenumber is not specified then file number zero (0) will be used.

 **New Concept**	`seek expression`
	`seek(expression)`
	`seek filenumber,expression`
	`seek (filenumber,expression)`
	
	Move the file pointer for the next read or write operation to a specific location in the file. To move the current pointer to the beginning of the file use the value zero (0). To seek to the end of a file use the **size**() function as the argument to the see statement.
	
	If filenumber is not specified then file number zero (0) will be used.

 **New Concept**	`writeline expression`
	`writeline(expression)`
	`writeline filenumber,expression`
	`writeline (filenumber,expression)`
	
	Output the contents of the expression to an open file and then append an end of line mark to the data. The file pointer will be positioned at the end of the write so that the next write statement will directly follow.
	
	If filenumber is not specified then file number zero (0) will be used.

```
1     # c17_appendwrite.kbs
2     # append new lines on the end of a file
3     # then display it
4
5     open "e2_c17_appendwrite.dat"
6
7     print "enter a blank line to close file"
```

```
8
9       # move file pointer to end of file and append
10      seek size
11      while true
12          input ">", l$
13          if l$ = "" then exit while
14          writeline l$
15      end while
16
17      # move file pointer to beginning and show contents
18      seek 0
19      k = 0
20      while not eof()
21          k = k + 1
22          print k + " " + readline()
23      end while
24
25      close
26      end
```

Program 112: Append Lines to a File

```
enter a blank line to close file
>sed sed sed
>vim vim vim
>
1 bar bar bar
2 foo foo foo
3 grap grap grap
4 sed sed sed
5 vim vim vim
```

Sample Output 112: Append Lines to a File

Read() Function and Write Statement:

In the first three programs of this chapter we have discussed the **readline**() function and **writeline** statement. There are two other statements that will read and write a file. They are the **read**() function and **write** statement.

```
read
read()
read(filenumber)
```

Read the next word or number (token) from a file. Tokens are delimited by spaces, tab characters, or end of lines. Multiple delimiters between tokens will be treated as one.

If filenumber is not specified then file number zero (0) will be used.

```
write expression
write (expression)
write filenumber,expression
write (filenumber,expression)
```

Write the string expression to a file file. Do not add an end of line or a delimiter.

If filenumber is not specified then file number zero (0) will be used.

Big Program

This program uses a single text file to help us maintain a list of our friend's telephone numbers.

```
1       # c17_phonelist.kbs
2       # add a phone number to the list and show
3
4       filename$ = "c17_phonelist.txt"
5
6       print "phonelist.kbs - Manage your phone list."
7       do
8          input "Add, List, Quit (a/l/q)? ",action$
9          if left(lower(action$),1) = "a" then call
       addrecord(filename$)
10         if left(lower(action$),1) = "l" then call
       listfile(filename$)
11      until left(lower(action$),1) = "q"
12      end
13
14      subroutine listfile(f$)
15         if exists(f$) then
16            # list the names and phone numbers in the file
17            open f$
18            print "the file is " + size + " bytes long"
19            while not eof
20               # read next line from file and print it
21               print readline
22            end while
23            close
24         else
25            print "No phones on file.  Add first."
26         end if
```

```
27    end subroutine
28
29    subroutine addrecord(f$)
30        input "Name to add? ", name$
31        input "Phone to add? ", phone$
32        open f$
33        # seek to the end of the file
34        seek size()
35        # we are at end of file - add new line
36        writeline name$ + ", " + phone$
37        close
38    end subroutine
```

Program 113: Big Program - Phone List

```
phonelist.kbs - Manage your phone list.
Add, List, Quit (a/l/q)? l
the file is 46 bytes long
jim, 555-5555
sam, 555-7777
doug, 555-3333
Add, List, Quit (a/l/q)? a
Name to add? ang
Phone to add? 555-0987
Add, List, Quit (a/l/q)? l
the file is 61 bytes long
jim, 555-5555
sam, 555-7777
doug, 555-3333
ang, 555-0987
Add, List, Quit (a/l/q)? q
```

Sample Output 113: Big Program - Phone List

Exercises:

Word Search

```
e  n  i  l  e  t  i  r  w  e
s  y  r  o  t  c  e  r  i  d
n  e  k  o  t  s  q  h  e  r
e  f  m  e  t  s  f  l  e  p
p  p  s  s  i  i  a  s  c
o  e  i  z  l  m  d  e  l  e
r  x  e  e  i  l  e  o  r  o
e  e  r  t  i  k  s  y  e  f
t  k  e  n  z  e  l  j  a  d
b  r  e  w  r  i  t  e  d  n
```

close, delimiter, directory, eof, exists, file, open, read, readline, reset, seek, size, token, write, writeline
words

Problems

17.1. Create a file in the directory where you save your programs named "numbers.txt". Open it with a text editor, like Notepad in Windows or gEdit in LINUX, and type in a list of decimal numbers. Put each one on a separate line.

Now write a program to read the numbers from the file, one line at a time. Calculate the total of the numbers in the file and the average.

Remember to use the **float()** function to convert the string you read from the file to a numeric value before you add it to the running total.

17.2. Create a file in the directory where you save your programs named "people.txt". Open it with a text editor, like Notepad in

Windows or gEdit in LINUX, and type in the data below.

```
Jim,M,47
Mary,F,23
Bob,M,67
John,M,13
Sue,F,18
```

Write a program that will read in the data from the people file. Use string handling functions from Chapter 16 to break each line into three parts: 1) name, 2) gender, and 3) age. Tally the total of the ages, the number of people, and the number of males as you read the file. Once you have read all of the records display the percentage of males and the average age of the people in the file.

17.3. Create a file in the directory where you save your programs named "assignments.txt". Open it with a text editor, like Notepad in Windows or gEdit in LINUX, and type in the data below.

```
Jim,88,45
Joe,90,33
Mary,54,29
Maury, 57,30
```

Write a program that will read in the data from the assignments file and write out a new file named "finalgrade.txt" with the student's name, a comma, and their course grade. Calculate the course grade for each student based on the two assignment grades. The first assignment was worth 100 points and the second assignment was worth 50 points.

The output should look something like:

```
Jim,88
...
```

Chapter 18: Stacks, Queues, Lists, and Sorting

This chapter introduces a few advanced topics that are commonly covered in the first Computer Science class at the University level. The first three topics (Stack, Queue, and Linked List) are very common ways that information is stored in a computer system. The last two are algorithms for sorting information.

Stack:

A stack is one of the common data structures used by programmers to do many tasks. A stack works like the "discard pile" when you play the card game "crazy-eights". When you add a piece of data to a stack it is done on the top (called a "push") and these items stack upon each other. When you want a piece of information you take the top one off the stack and reveal the next one down (called a "pop"). Illustration 31 shows a graphical example.

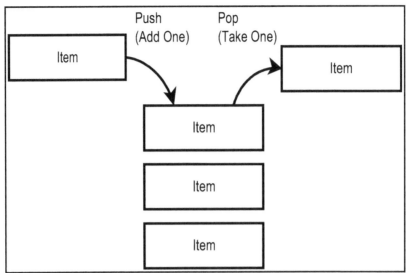

Illustration 31: What is a Stack

The operation of a stack can also be described as "last-in, first-out" or LIFO for short. The most recent item added will be the next item removed. Program 114 implements a stack using an array and a pointer to the most recently added item. In the "push" subroutine you will see array logic that will re-dimension the array to make sure there is enough room available in the stack for virtually any number of items to be added.

```
1     # c18_stack.kbs
2     # implementing a stack using an array
3
4     dim stack(1) # array to hold stack with initial size
5     nstack = 0 # number of elements on stack
6     global stack, nstack
7
8     call push(1)
9     call push(2)
10    call push(3)
11    call push(4)
12    call push(5)
13
```

```
14    while not empty()
15    print pop()
16    end while
17
18    end
19
20    function empty()
21    # return true if the start is empty
22    return nstack=0
23    end function
24
25    function pop()
26    # get the top number from stack and return it
27    # or print a message and return -1
28    if nstack = 0 then
29    print "stack empty"
30    return -1
31    end if
32    nstack = nstack - 1
33    value = stack[nstack]
34    return value
35    end function
36
37    subroutine push(value)
38    # push the number in the variable value onto the
      stack
39    # make the stack larger if it is full
40    if nstack = stack[?] then redim stack(stack[?] + 5)
41    stack[nstack] = value
42    nstack = nstack + 1
43    end subroutine
```

Program 114: Stack

```
5
4
3
2
1
```

Sample Output 114: Stack

```
global variable
global variable, variable...
```

Global tells BASIC-256 that these variables can be seen by the entire program (both inside and outside the functions/subroutines). Using global variables is typically not encouraged, but when there is the need to share several values or arrays it may be appropriate.

Queue:

The queue (pronounced like the letter Q) is another very common data structure. The queue, in its simplest form, is like the lunch line at school. The first one in the line is the first one to get to eat. Illustration 32 shows a block diagram of a queue.

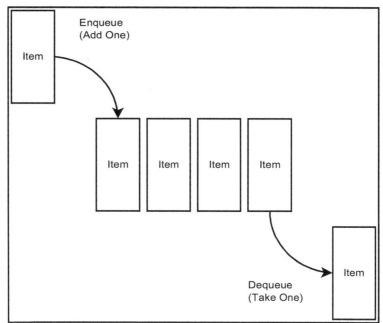

Illustration 32: What is a Queue

The terms enqueue (pronounced in-q) and dequeue (pronounced dee-q) are the names we use to describe adding a new item to the end of the line (tail) or removing an item from the front of the line (head). Sometimes this is described as a "first-in, first-out" or FIFO. The example in Program 115 uses an array and two pointers that keep track of the head of the line and the tail of the line.

```
1      # c18_queue.kbs
2      # implementing a queue using an array
3
4      global queuesize, queue, queuetail, queuehead,
       inqueue
5
6      call createqueue(5)
7
8      call enqueue(1)
9      call enqueue(2)
```

```
10
11    print dequeue()
12    print
13
14    call enqueue(3)
15    call enqueue(4)
16
17    print dequeue()
18    print dequeue()
19    print
20
21    call enqueue(5)
22    call enqueue(6)
23    call enqueue(7)
24
25    # empty everybody from the queue
26    while inqueue > 0
27       print dequeue()
28    end while
29
30    end
31
32    subroutine createqueue(z)
33       # maximum number of entries in the queue at any
      one time
34       queuesize = z
35       # array to hold queue with initial size
36       dim queue(z)
37       # location in queue of next new entry
38       queuetail = 0
39       # location in queue of next entry to be returned
      (served)
40       queuehead = 0
41       # number of entries in queue
42       inqueue = 0
43    end subroutine
44
45    function dequeue()
46       if inqueue = 0 then
```

```
47              print "queue is empty"
48              value = -1
49           else
50              value = queue[queuehead]
51              inqueue--
52              queuehead++
53              if queuehead = queuesize then queuehead = 0
54           end if
55           return value
56        end function
57
58        subroutine enqueue(value)
59           if inqueue = queuesize then
60              print "queue is full"
61           else
62              queue[queuetail] = value
63              inqueue++
64              queuetail++
65              if queuetail = queuesize then queuetail = 0
66           end if
67        end subroutine
```

Program 115: Queue

```
1
2
3

4
5
6
7
```

Sample Output 115: Queue

Linked List:

In most books the discussion of this material starts with the linked list. Because BASIC-256 handles memory differently than many other languages this discussion was saved after introducing stacks and queues.

A linked list is a sequence of nodes that contains data and a pointer or index to the next node in the list. In addition to the nodes with their information we also need a pointer to the first node. We call the first node the "Head". Take a look at Illustration 33 and you will see how each node points to another.

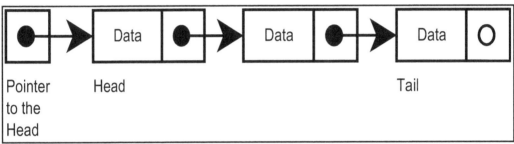

Illustration 33: Linked List

An advantage to the linked list, over an array, is the ease of inserting or deleting a node. To delete a node all you need to do is change the pointer on the previous node (Illustration 34) and release the discarded node so that it may be reused.

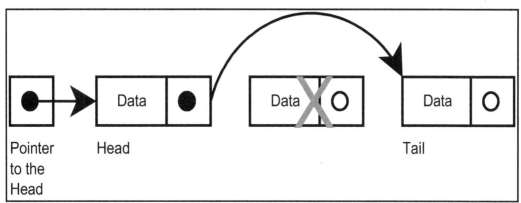

Illustration 34: Deleting an Item from a Linked List

Inserting a new node is also as simple as creating the new node, linking the new node to the next node, and linking the previous node to the first node. Illustration 35 Shows inserting a new node into the second position.

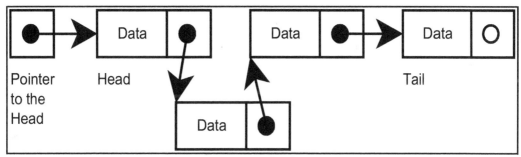

Illustration 35: Inserting an Item into a Linked List

Linked lists are commonly thought of as the simplest data structures. In the BASIC language we can't allocate memory like in most languages so we will simulate this behavior using arrays. In Program 116 we use the data$ array to store the text in the list, the nextitem array to contain the index to the next node, and the freeitem array to contain a stack of free (unused) array indexes.

```
1      # c18_linkedlist.kbs
2
3      # create a linked list using arrays
4
5      # data$ is an array coitaining the data strings in
       the list
6      # nextitem is an array with pointers to the next data
       item
7      # if nextitem is -2 it is free or -1 it is the end
8
9      global head, data$, nextitem
10     call initialize(6)
11
12     # list of 3 people
13     call append("Bob")
14     call append("Sue")
15     call append("Guido")
16     call displaylist()
17     call displayarrays()
18     call wait()
19
20     print "delete person 2"
21     call delete(2)
22     call displaylist()
23     call displayarrays()
24     call wait()
25
26     print "insert Mary into the front of the list (#1)"
27     call insert("Mary",1)
28     call displaylist()
29     call displayarrays()
30     call wait()
31
32     print "insert John at position 2"
33     call insert("John",2)
34     call displaylist()
35     call displayarrays()
36     call wait()
37
```

```
38    print "delete person 1"
39    call delete(1)
40    call displaylist()
41    call displayarrays()
42    call wait()
43
44    end
45
46    subroutine wait()
47       input "press enter to continue> ",foo$
48       print
49    end subroutine
50
51    subroutine initialize(n)
52       head = -1     # start of list (-1 pointer to
      nowhere)
53       dim data$(n)
54       dim nextitem(n)
55       # initialize items as free
56       for t = 0 to data$[?]-1
57          call freeitem(t)
58       next t
59    end subroutine
60
61    subroutine freeitem(i)
62       # free element at array index i
63       data$[i] = ""
64       nextitem[i] = -2
65    end subroutine
66
67    function findfree()
68       # find a free item (an item pointing to -2)
69       for t = 0 to data$[?]-1
70          if nextitem[t] = -2 then return t
71       next t
72       print 'no free elements to allocate'
73       end
74    end function
75
```

```
76     function createitem(text$)
77        # create a new item on the list
78        # and return index to new location
79        i = findfree()
80        data$[i] = text$
81        nextitem[i] = -1
82        return i
83     end function
84
85     subroutine displaylist()
86        # showlist by following the linked list
87        print "list..."
88        k = 0
89        i = head
90        do
91           k = k + 1
92           print k + " ";
93           print data$[i]
94           i = nextitem[i]
95        until i = -1
96     end subroutine
97
98     subroutine displayarrays()
99        # show data actually stored and how
100       print "arrays..."
101       for i = 0 to data$[?]-1
102          print i + " " + data$[i] + " >" + nextitem[i]  ;
103          if head = i then print " <<head";
104          print
105       next i
106    end subroutine
107
108    subroutine insert(text$, n)
109       # insert text$ at position n
110       index = createitem(text$)
111       if n = 1 then
112          nextitem[index] = head
113          head = index
114       else
```

```
115            k = 2
116            i = head
117            while i <> -1 and k <> n
118               k = k + 1
119               i = nextitem[i]
120            end while
121            if i <> -1 then
122               nextitem[index] = nextitem[i]
123               nextitem[i] = index
124            else
125               print "can't insert beyond end of list"
126            end if
127         end if
128      end subroutine
129
130      subroutine delete(n)
131         # delete element n from linked list
132         if n = 1 then
133            # delete head - make second element the new
         head
134            index = head
135            head = nextitem[index]
136            call freeitem(index)
137         else
138            k = 2
139            i = head
140            while i <> -1 and k <> n
141               k = k + 1
142               i = nextitem[i]
143            end while
144            if i <> -1 then
145               index = nextitem[i]
146               nextitem[i] = nextitem[nextitem[i]]
147               call freeitem(index)
148            else
149               print "can't delete beyond end of list"
150            end if
151         end if
152      end subroutine
```

```
153
154   subroutine append(text$)
155      # append  text$ to end of linked list
156      index = createitem(text$)
157      if head = -1 then
158         # no head yet - make item the head
159         head = index
160      else
161         # move to the end of the list and add new item
162         i = head
163         while nextitem[i] <> -1
164            i = nextitem[i]
165         end while
166         nextitem[i] = index
167      endif
168   end subroutine
```

Program 116: Linked List

Explore

Re-write Program 116 to implement a stack and a queue using a linked list.

Slow and Inefficient Sort - Bubble Sort:

The "Bubble Sort" is probably the worst algorithm ever devised to sort a list of values. It is very slow and inefficient except for small sets of items. This is a classic example of a bad algorithm.

The only real positive thing that can be said about this algorithm is that it is simple to explain and to implement. Illustration 36 shows a flow-chart of the algorithm. The bubble sort goes through the array over and over again swapping the order of adjacent items until the sort is complete,

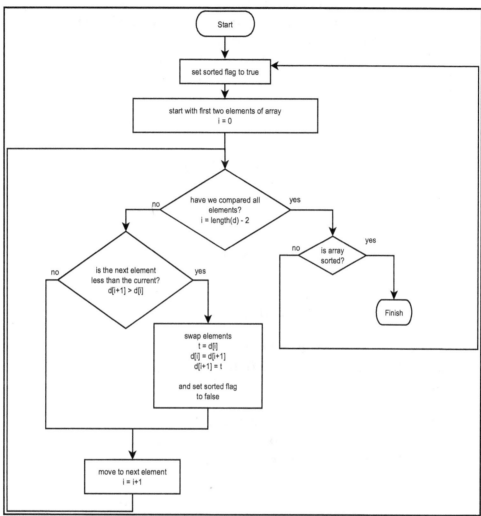

Illustration 36: Bubble Sort - Flowchart

```
1    # c18_bubblesortf.kbs
2    # implementing a simple sort
3
4    # a bubble sort is one of the SLOWEST algorithms
```

```
5      # for sorting but it is the easiest to implement
6      # and understand.
7      #
8      # The algorithm for a bubble sort is
9      # 1. Go through the array swaping adjacent values
10     #    so that lower value comes first.
11     # 2. Do step 1 over and over until there have
12     #    been no swaps (the array is sorted)
13     #
14
15     dim d(20)
16
17     # fill array with unsorted numbers
18     for i = 0 to d[?]-1
19        d[i] = int(rand * 1000)
20     next i
21
22     print "*** Un-Sorted ***"
23
24     call displayarray(ref(d))
25     call bubblesort(ref(d))
26
27     print "*** Sorted ***"
28     call displayarray(ref(d))
29     end
30
31     subroutine displayarray(ref(array))
32        # print out the array's values
33        for i = 0 to array[?]-1
34           print array[i] + " ";
35        next i
36        print
37     end subroutine
38
39     subroutine bubblesort(ref(array))
40        do
41           sorted = true
42           for i = 0 to array[?] - 2
43              if array[i] > array[i+1] then
```

```
44              sorted = false
45              temp = array[i+1]
46              array[i+1] = array[i]
47              array[i] = temp
48           end if
49        next i
50     until sorted
51  end subroutine
```

Program 117: Bubble Sort

```
*** Un-Sorted ***
878 95 746 345 750 232 355 472 649 678 758 424
653 698 482 154 91 69 895 414
*** Sorted ***
69 91 95 154 232 345 355 414 424 472 482 649
653 678 698 746 750 758 878 895
```

Sample Output 117: Bubble Sort

Better Sort – Insertion Sort:

The insertion sort is another algorithm for sorting a list of items. It is usually faster than the bubble sort, but in the worst case case could take as long.

The insertion sort gets it's name from how it works. The sort goes through the elements of the array (index = 1 to length -1) and inserts the value in the correct location in the previous array elements. Illustration 37 shows a step-by-step example.

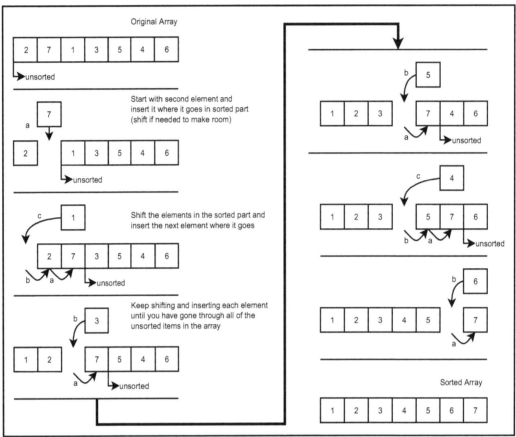

Illustration 37: Insertion Sort - Step-by-step

```
1    # c18_insertionsort.kbs
2    # implementing an efficient sort
3
4    # The insertion sort loops through the items
5    # starting at the second element.
6
7    # takes current element and inserts it
8    # in the the correct sorted place in
9    # the previously sorted elements
10
11   # moving from backward from the current
12   # location and sliding elements with a
```

```
13       # larger value forward to make room for
14       # the current value in the correct
15       # place (in the partially sorted array)
16
17       dim d(20)
18
19       # fill array with unsorted numbers
20       for i = 0 to d[?]-1
21          d[i] = int(rand * 1000)
22       next i
23
24       print "*** Un-Sorted ***"
25       call displayarray(ref(d))
26
27       call insertionsort(ref(d))
28
29       print "*** Sorted ***"
30       call displayarray(ref(d))
31       end
32
33       subroutine displayarray(ref(a))
34          # print out the array's values
35          for i = 0 to a[?]-1
36             print a[i] + " ";
37          next i
38          print
39       end subroutine
40
41       subroutine insertionsort(ref(a))
42          for i = 1 to a[?] - 1
43             currentvalue = a[i]
44             j = i - 1
45             done = false
46             do
47                if a[j] > currentvalue then
48                   a[j+1] = a[j]
49                   j = j - 1
50                   if j < 0 then done = true
51                else
```

```
52                      done = true
53                  endif
54            until done
55            a[j+1] = currentvalue
56        next i
57    end subroutine
```

Program 118: Insertion Sort


```
*** Un-Sorted ***
913 401 178 844 574 289 583 806 332 835 439 52
140 802 365 972 898 737 297 65
*** Sorted ***
52 65 140 178 289 297 332 365 401 439 574 583
737 802 806 835 844 898 913 972
```

Sample Output 118: Insertion Sort

Exercises:

Word Search

```
k f i f o e q i q h m t o
n o f i l u x q q y e r b
i h p v e o d t q y u o d
l m p u f d s r c t e s e
v o e k x v m o i s u n u
p g f c i l e s a i q o e
q l f a u h m e l l n i u
v o i t q s o l l i e t q
i b c s z u r b o d t r e
z a i v e p y b c s z e d
d l e y d j h u a r o s p
z y n g o v c b t y l n q
m x t s n y i t e i q i b
```

allocate, bubblesort, dequeue, efficient, enqueue, fifo, global, insertionsort, lifo, link, list, memory, node, pop, push, queue, stack

Problems

18.1. Rewrite the "Bubble Sort" function to sort strings, not numbers. Add a second true/false argument to make the sort case sensitive/insensitive.

18.2. Implement the "Insertion Sort" using the linked-list functions so that items are moved logically and not physically moved.

18.3. Develop a function to do the "Merge Sort" (http://en.wikipedia.org/wiki/Merge_sort) on an array of numbers. Create arrays of random numbers of varying lengths ans sotrt them using the "Bubble Sort", the "Insertion Sort", and your new "Merge Sort". Which is the slowest? Fastest?

Chapter 19 – Runtime Error Trapping

As you have worked through the examples and created your own programs you have seen errors that happen while the program is running. These errors are called "runtime errors". BASIC-256 includes a group of special commands that allow your program to recover from or handle these errors.

You may already have seen programs that throw or display errors when they are running. They often occur when an invalid mathematical operation happens or when an unassigned variable is used. In Program 119 you see a program that works most of the time but will error and quit running if the denominator is zero.

```
1     # c19_divider.kbs
2     # simple division
3
4     print "divide two numbers"
5     while true
6        input "numerator?", n
7        input "denominator?", d
8        q = n/d
9        print "quotient is  " + q
10    end while
```

Program 119: Simple Division Program That May Error

```
divide two numbers
numerator?6
denominator?9
quotient is  0.6666667
numerator?5
denominator?2
quotient is  2.5
numerator?9
```

```
denominator?0
ERROR on line 8: Division by zero.
```
Sample Output 119: Simple Division Program That May Error

Try a Statement and Catch an Error:

The **try/catch/end try** block is structured so that if a trappable runtime error occurs in the code between the **try** and the **catch**, the code immediately following the **catch** will be executed. The following example shows the simple division program now catching the division by zero error.

```
1      # c19_trycatch.kbs
2      # simple try catch
3
4      print "divide two numbers"
5      while true
6         input "numerator?", n
7         input "denominator?", d
8         try
9            q = n/d
10           print "quotient is  " + q
11        catch
12           print "I can't divide " + d + " into " + n
13        end try
14     end while
```

Program 120: Simple Division Program That Catches Error


```
divide two numbers
numerator?5
denominator?6
quotient is   0.8333333
numerator?99
denominator?0
I can't divide 0 into 99
numerator?4
```

```
denominator?3
quotient is  1.3333333
numerator?
```
Sample Output 120: Simple Division Program That Catches Error

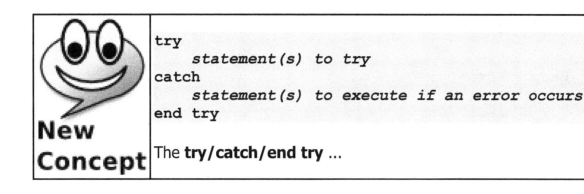

```
try
     statement(s) to try
catch
     statement(s) to execute if an error occurs
end try
```

New Concept The **try/catch/end try** ...

Trapping errors, when you do not mean too, can cause problems and mask other problems with your programs. Error trapping should only be used when needed and disabled when not.

Finding Out Which Error:

Sometimes just knowing that an error happened is not enough. There are functions that will return the error number (**lasterror**), the line where the error happened in the program (**lasterrorline**), a text message describing the error (**lasterrormessage**), and extra command specific error messages (**lasterrorextra**).

```
1    # c19_trap.kbs
2    # error trapping with reporting
3
4    try
5       print "z = " + z
```

```
 6      catch
 7         print "Caught Error"
 8         print "   Error = " + lasterror
 9         print "   On Line = " + lasterrorline
10         print "   Message = " + lasterrormessage
11      end try
12      print "Still running after error"
```
Program 121: Try/Catch - With Messages


```
Caught Error
   Error = 12
   On Line = 4
   Message = Unknown variable z
Still running after error
```
Sample Output 121: Try/Catch - With Messages

New Concept

```
lasterror or lasterror()
lasterrorline or lasterrorline()
lasterrormessage or lasterrormessage()
lasterrorextra or lasterrorextra()
```

The four "last error" functions will return information about the last trapped error. These values will remain unchanged until another error is encountered.

lasterror	Returns the number of the last trapped error. If no errors have been trapped this function will return a zero. See Appendix G: Errors and Warnings for a complete list of trappable errors.
lasterrorline	Returns the line number, of the program, where the last error was trapped.
lasterrormessage	Returns a string describing the last error.
lasterrorextra	Returns a string with additional error information. For most errors this function will not return any information.

Type Conversion Errors

BASIC-256 by default will return a zero when it is unable to convert a string to a number. You may have seen this back in Chapter 5 when using the **input** statement. This will also happen when the **int()** and **float()** functions convert a string to a number.

You may optionally tell BASIC-256 to display a trappable warning or throw an error that stops execution of your program. You can change this setting in the "Preferences" dialog, on the User tab.

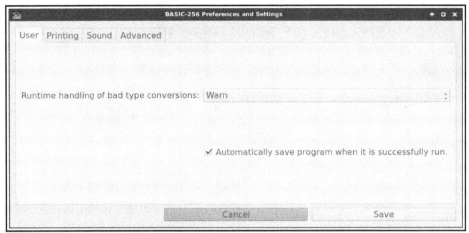

Illustration 38: Preferences - Type Conversion Ignore/Warn/Error

```
1       # c19_inputnumber.kbs
2
3       input "enter a number> ",a
4       print a
```

Program 122: Type Conversion Error

Program run with the errors "Ignored".

```
enter a number> foo
0
```

Sample Output 122: Type Conversion Error - Ignored (Deafult)

Program run with the "Warning" enabled. Notice that the program continues running but displays a message. The **try/catch/end try** statements will catch the warning so that you may display a custom message or do special proccessing.

```
enter a number> sdfsdf
WARNING on line 3: Unable to convert string to
number, zero used.
```

> 0

Sample Output 122: Type Conversion Error - Warning

This third example had the property set to "Error". When an invalid type conversion happens an error is displayed and program execution stops. This error is trappable with the **try/catch/end try** statements.

```
enter a number> abcd
ERROR on line 3: Unable to convert string to
number.
```

Sample Output 122: Type Conversion Error - Error

Creating An Error Trapping Routine:

There is a second way to trap run-time errors, by using an error trapping subroutine. When this type of error trapping is turned on, with the **onerror** statement, the program will call a specified subroutine when an error occurs. When the error trap returns the program will automatically continue with the next line in the program.

If we look at Program 123 we will see that the program calls the subroutine when it tries to read the value of z (an undefined variable). If we try to run the same program with line one commented out or removed the program will terminate when the error happens.

```
1    # c19_simpletrap.kbs
2    # simple error trapping
3
4    onerror trap
5
6    print "z = " + z
7    print "Still running after error"
8    end
```

```
9
10     subroutine trap()
11        print "I trapped an error."
12     end subroutine
```
Program 123: Simple Runtime Error Trap


```
I trapped an error.
z = 0
Still running after error
```
Sample Output 123: Simple Runtime Error Trap

onerror label

Create an error trap that will automatically jump to the subroutine at the specified label when an error occurs.

New Concept

You may use the **lasterror, lasterrorline, lasterrormessage,** and **lasterrorextra** functions within your error trap subroutine to display any messages or do any processing you wish to do. Additionally you may not define an **onerror** trap inside a **try/catch**.

Turning Off Error Trapping Routine:

Sometimes in a program we will want to trap errors during part of the program and not trap other errors. The **offerror** statement turns error trapping off. This causes all errors encountered to stop the program.


```
1       # c19_trapoff.kbs
```

```
2       # error trapping with reporting
3
4       onerror errortrap
5       print "z = " + z
6       print "Still running after first error"
7
8       offerror
9       print "z = " + z
10      print "Still running after second error"
11      end
12
13      subroutine errortrap()
14          print "Error Trap - Activated"
15      end subroutine
```
Program 124: Turning Off the Trap

```
Error Trap - Activated
z = 0
Still running after first error
ERROR on line 6: Unknown variable
```
Sample Output 124: Turning Off the Trap

Exercises:

Word Search

```
e u q r l w f e p j x s p w n c
p g u b i r r h f j w w w o c p
b l a s t e r r o r e x t r a p
q e e s v w j l p g a m w l o q
t a n n s r q o i i t m r a n o
r f x i d e o u c a t c h t e y
y h z r l t m r f k o s k v r i
q o i b m r r r s i e f b r f
x l f x o z o y o e l b b i o a
y k m f z o r r q r t s k e r a
z a h l e i r y r p r s f g y m
i l i l n r e j f e p e a n r l
a q c m t q r k o g t l t l u u
r e u k z b b o u f l s g s t j
m s u h l a r x r m v w a q a l
u b z r l h a l k p a r t l n l
```

catch, endtry, error, lasterror, lasterrorextra, lasterrorline, lasterrormessage, offerror, onerror, trap, try

Problems

19.1. Set the "runtime handling of bad type conversion" "Preference" to "warn" or "Error" and write a simple program that asks the user to enter a number. If the user enters something that is not a number, trap the warning/error and ask again.

```
enter a number> gdf2345
bad entry. try again.
enter a number> fdg545
bad entry. try again.
enter a number> 43fdgdf
bad entry. try again.
```

```
          enter a number> 22
          You entered 22
```

19.2. Take the logic you just developed in Problem 19.1 and create a function that takes one argument, the prompt message, repeatedly asks the user for a number until they enter one, and returns the user's numeric entry.

19.3. Write a program that causes many errors to occur, trap and them. Be sure to check out Appendix G: Errors and Warnings for a complete list

Chapter 20: Database Programming

This chapter will show how BASIC-256 can connect to a simple relational database and use it to store and retrieve useful information.

What is a Database:

A database is simply an organized collection of numbers, string, and other types of information. The most common type of database is the "Relational Database". Relational Databases are made up of four major parts: tables, rows, columns, and relationships (see Table 9).

Table	A table consists of a predefined number or columns any any number of rows with information about a specific object or subject. Also known as a relation.
Row	Also called a tuple.
Column	This can also be referred to as an attribute.
Relationship	A reference of the key of one table as a column of another table. This creates a connection between tables.

Table 9: Major Components of a Relational Database

The SQL Language:

Most relational databases, today, use a language called SQL to actually extract and manipulate data. SQL is actually an acronym for Structured Query Language. The original SQL language was developed by IBM in the 1970s and has become the primary language used by relational databases.

SQL is a very powerful language and has been implemented by dozens of software companies, over the years. Because of this complexity there are many different dialects of SQL in use. BASIC-256 uses the SQLite database engine. Please see the SQLite web-page at http://www.sqlite.org for more information about the dialect of SQL shown in these examples.

Creating and Adding Data to a Database:

The SQLite library does not require the installation of a database sever or the setting up of a complex system. The database and all of its parts are stored in a simple file on your computer. This file can even be copied to another computer and used, without problem.

The first program (Program 125: Create a Database) creates a new sample database file and tables. The tables are represented by the Entity Relationship Diagram (ERD) as shown in Illustration 39.

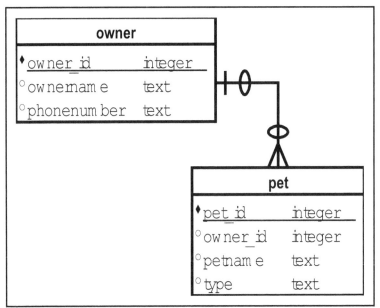

Illustration 39: Entity Relationship Diagram of Chapter Database

```
1      # c20_createpetsdb.kbs
2      # create the "pets.sqlite" data base
3
4      # delete old database if it exists
5      file$ = "pets.sqlite3"
6      if exists(file$) then kill(file$)
7
8      # open database file
9      dbopen file$
10
11     stmt$ =  "CREATE TABLE owner (owner_id INTEGER,
       ownername TEXT, phonenumber TEXT, PRIMARY KEY
       (owner_id));"
12     print stmt$
13     dbexecute stmt$
14
15     stmt$ =  "CREATE TABLE pet (pet_id INTEGER, owner_id
       INTEGER, petname TEXT, type TEXT, PRIMARY KEY
       (pet_id), FOREIGN KEY (owner_id) REFERENCES owner
       (owner_id));"
16     print stmt$
17     dbexecute stmt$
18
19     dbclose
20     print file$ + " created."
21     end
```

Program 125: Create a Database

```
CREATE TABLE owner (owner_id INTEGER, ownername
TEXT, phonenumber TEXT, PRIMARY KEY
(owner_id));
CREATE TABLE pet (pet_id INTEGER, owner_id
INTEGER, petname TEXT, type TEXT, PRIMARY KEY
(pet_id), FOREIGN KEY (owner_id) REFERENCES
owner (owner_id));
```

```
pets.sqlite3 created.
```

Sample Output 125: Create a Database

So far you have seen three new database statements: **dbopen** – will open a database file and create it if it does not exist, **dbexecute** – will execute an SQL statement on the open database, and **dbclose** – closes the open database file.

dbopen filename

Open an SQLite database file. If the database does not exist then create a new empty database file.

dbexecute sqlstatement

Perform the SQL statement on the currently open SQLite database file. No value will be returned but a trappable runtime error will occur if there were any problems executing the statement on the database.

dbclose

Close the currently open SQLite database file. This statement insures that all data is written out to the database file.

New Concept

These same three statements can also be used to execute other SQL statements. The INSERT INTO statement (Program 126) adds new rows of data to the tables and the UPDATE statement (Program 127) will change an existing row's information.

```
1    # c20_addpetsdb.kbs
2    # add rows to the database
3
4    file$ = "pets.sqlite3"
5    dbopen file$
6
7    call addowner(1, "Jim", "555-3434")
8    call addpet(1, 1, "Spot", "Cat")
9    call addpet(2, 1, "Fred", "Cat")
10   call addpet(3, 1, "Elvis", "Cat")
11
12   call addowner(2, "Sue", "555-8764")
13   call addpet(4, 2, "Alfred", "Dog")
14   call addpet(5, 2, "Fido", "Cat")
15
16   call addowner(3, "Amy", "555-4321")
17   call addpet(6, 3, "Bones", "Dog")
18
19   call addowner(4, "Dee", "555-9659")
20   call addpet(7, 4, "Sam", "Goat")
21
```

```
22      # wrap everything up
23      dbclose
24      end
25
26      subroutine addowner(owner_id, ownername$,
        phonenumber$)
27         stmt$ = "INSERT INTO owner (owner_id, ownername,
        phonenumber) VALUES (" + owner_id + "," + chr(34) +
        ownername$ + chr(34) + "," + chr(34) + phonenumber$ +
        chr(34) + ");"
28         print stmt$
29         try
30            dbexecute stmt$
31         catch
32            print "Unbale to add owner " + owner_id + " " +
        lasterrorextra
33         end try
34      end subroutine
35
36      subroutine addpet(pet_id, owner_id, petname$, type$)
37         stmt$ = "INSERT INTO pet (pet_id, owner_id,
        petname, type) VALUES (" + pet_id + "," + owner_id +
        "," + chr(34) + petname$ + chr(34) + "," + chr(34) +
        type$ + chr(34) + ");"
38         print stmt$
39         try
40            dbexecute stmt$
41         catch
42            print "Unbale to add pet " + pet_id + " " +
        lasterrorextra
43         end try
44      endsubroutine
```

Program 126: Insert Rows into Database

```
INSERT INTO owner (owner_id, ownername,
phonenumber) VALUES (1,"Jim","555-3434");
```

```
INSERT INTO pet (pet_id, owner_id, petname,
type) VALUES (1,1,"Spot","Cat");
INSERT INTO pet (pet_id, owner_id, petname,
type) VALUES (2,1,"Fred","Cat");
INSERT INTO pet (pet_id, owner_id, petname,
type) VALUES (3,1,"Elvis","Cat");
INSERT INTO owner (owner_id, ownername,
phonenumber) VALUES (2,"Sue","555-8764");
INSERT INTO pet (pet_id, owner_id, petname,
type) VALUES (4,2,"Alfred","Dog");
INSERT INTO pet (pet_id, owner_id, petname,
type) VALUES (5,2,"Fido","Cat");
INSERT INTO owner (owner_id, ownername,
phonenumber) VALUES (3,"Amy","555-4321");
INSERT INTO pet (pet_id, owner_id, petname,
type) VALUES (6,3,"Bones","Dog");
INSERT INTO owner (owner_id, ownername,
phonenumber) VALUES (4,"Dee","555-9659");
INSERT INTO pet (pet_id, owner_id, petname,
type) VALUES (7,4,"Sam","Goat");
```

Sample Output 126: Insert Rows into Database

```
1      # c20_updatepetsdb.kbs
2      # update a database row
3
4      dbopen "pets.sqlite3"
5
6      # create and populate
7      s$ =  "UPDATE owner SET phonenumber = " + chr(34) +
       "555-5555" + chr(34) + " where owner_id = 1;"
8      print s$
9      dbexecute s$
10     dbclose
```

Program 127: Update Row in a Database

```
UPDATE owner SET phonenumber = "555-5555" where
owner_id = 1;
```

Sample Output 127: Update Row in a Database

Retrieving Information from a Database:

So far we have seen how to open, close, and execute a SQL statement that does not return any values. A database would be pretty useless if we could not get information out of it.

The SELECT statement, in the SQL language, allows us to retrieve the desired data. After a SELECT is executed a "record set" is created that contains the rows and columns of data that was extracted from the database. Program 128 shows three different SELECT statements and how the data is read into your BASIC-256 program.

```
1     # c20_showpetsdb.kbs
2     # display data from the pets database
3
4     dbopen "pets.sqlite3"
5
6     # show owners and their phone numbers
7     print "Owners and Phone Numbers"
8     dbopenset "SELECT ownername, phonenumber FROM owner
      ORDER BY ownername;"
9     while dbrow()
10       print dbstring(0) + " " + dbstring(1)
11    end while
12    dbcloseset
13
14    print
15
16    # show owners and their pets
17    print "Owners with Pets"
```

```
18      dbopenset "SELECT owner.ownername, pet.pet_id,
        pet.petname, pet.type FROM owner JOIN pet ON
        pet.owner_id = owner.owner_id ORDER BY ownername,
        petname;"
19      while dbrow()
20         print dbstring(0) + " " + dbint(1) + " " +
        dbstring(2) + " " + dbstring(3)
21      end while
22      dbcloseset
23
24      print
25
26      # show average number of pets
27      print "Average Number of Pets"
28      dbopenset "SELECT AVG(c) FROM (SELECT COUNT(*) AS c
        FROM owner JOIN pet ON pet.owner_id = owner.owner_id
        GROUP BY owner.owner_id) AS numpets;"
29      while dbrow()
30         print dbfloat(0)
31      end while
32      dbcloseset
33
34      # wrap everything up
35      dbclose
```

Program 128: Selecting Sets of Data from a Database

```
Owners and Phone Numbers
Amy 555-9932
Dee 555-4433
Jim 555-5555
Sue 555-8764

Owners with Pets
Amy 6 Bones Dog
Dee 7 Sam Goat
Jim 3 Elvis Cat
Jim 2 Fred Cat
```

```
Jim 1 Spot Cat
Sue 4 Alfred Cat
Sue 5 Fido Dog

Average Number of Pets
1.75
```

Sample Output 128: Selecting Sets of Data from a Database

dbopenset sqlstatement

Execute a SELECT statement on the database and create a "record set" to allow the program to read in the result. The "record set" may contain 0 or more rows as extracted by the SELECT.

dbrow   or   dbrow ()

Function to advance the result of the last **dbopenset** to the next row. Returns false if we are at the end of the selected data.

You need to advance to the first row, using **dbrow**, after a **dbopenset** statement before you can read any data.

New Concept

```
dbint ( column )
dbfloat ( column )
dbstring ( column )
```

These functions will return data from the current row of the record set. You must know the zero based numeric column number of the desired data.

dbint	Return the cell data as an integer.
dbfloat	Return the cell data as a floating point number.
dbstring	Return the cell data as a string.

New Concept

```
dbcloseset
```

Close and discard the results of the last **dbopenset** statement.

Big Program

The big program this chapter creates a single program that creates, maintains, and lists phone numbers stored in a database file.

Pay special attention to the quote$ function used in creating the SQL statements. It wraps all strings in the statements in single quotes after changing the single quotes in a string to a pair of them. This doubling of quotes inside quotes is how to insert a quotation mark in an SQL statement.

```
1     # c20_rolofile.kbs
2     # a database example to keep track of phone numbers
3
4     dbopen "rolofile.sqlite3"
5     call createtables()
6
7     do
8        print
9        print "rolofile - phone numbers"
10       print "1-add person"
11       print "2-list people"
12       print "3-add phone"
13       print "4-list phones"
14       input "0-exit >", choice
15       print
16
17       if choice=1 then call addperson()
18       if choice=2 then call listpeople()
19       if choice=3 then call addphone()
20       if choice=4 then call listphone()
21    until choice = 0
22    dbclose
23    end
24
25    function quote$(a$)
26       # wrap a string in single quotes (for a sql
      statement)
27       # if it contains a single quote double it
28       return "'" + replace(a$,"'","''") + "'"
29    end function
30
31    function inputphonetype$()
32       do
33          input "Phone Type (h-home, c-cell, f-fax, w-
      work) > ", type$
34       until type$ = "h" or type$ = "c" or type$ = "f" or
      type$ = "w"
35       return type$
```

```
36    end function
37
38    subroutine createtables()
39       # includes the IF NOT EXISTS clause to not error
    if the
40       # table already exists
41       dbexecute "CREATE TABLE IF NOT EXISTS person
    (person_id TEXT PRIMARY KEY, name TEXT);"
42       dbexecute "CREATE TABLE IF NOT EXISTS phone
    (person_id TEXT, phone TEXT, type TEXT, PRIMARY KEY
    (person_id, phone));"
43    end subroutine
44
45    subroutine addperson()
46       print "add person"
47       input "person id > ", person_id$
48       person_id$ = upper(person_id$)
49       if ispersononfile(person_id$) or person_id$ = ""
    then
50          print "person already on file or empty"
51       else
52          input "person name > ", person_name$
53          if person_name$ = "" then
54             print "please enter name"
55          else
56             dbexecute "INSERT INTO person (person_id,
    name) VALUES (" + quote$(person_id$) + "," + quote$
    (person_name$) + ");"
57             print person_id$ + " added."
58          end if
59       end if
60    end subroutine
61
62    subroutine addphone()
63       print "add phone number"
64       input "person id > ", person_id$
65       person_id$ = upper(person_id$)
66       if not ispersononfile(person_id$) then
67          print "person not on file"
```

```
68          else
69              input "phone number > ", phone$
70              if phone$ = "" then
71                  print "please enter a phone number"
72              else
73                  type$ = inputphonetype$()
74                  dbexecute "INSERT INTO phone (person_id,
    phone, type) values (" + quote$(person_id$) + "," +
    quote$(phone$) + "," + quote$(type$) + ");"
75                  print phone$ + " added."
76              end if
77          end if
78      end subroutine
79
80      function ispersononfile(person_id$)
81          # return true/false whether the person is on the
    person table
82          onfile = false
83          dbopenset "select person_id from person where
    person_id = " + quote$(person_id$)
84          if dbrow() then onfile = true
85          dbcloseset
86          return onfile
87      end function
88
89      subroutine listpeople()
90          dbopenset "select person_id, name from person
    order by person_id"
91          while dbrow()
92              print dbstring("person_id") + " " +
    dbstring("name")
93          end while
94          dbcloseset
95      end subroutine
96
97      subroutine listphone()
98          input "person id to list (return for all) > ",
    person_id$
99          person_id$ = upper(person_id$)
```

```
100        stmt$ = "SELECT person.person_id, person.name,
      phone.phone, phone.type FROM person LEFT JOIN phone
      ON person.person_id = phone.person_id"
101        if person_id$ <> "" then stmt$ += " WHERE
      person.person_id = " + quote$(person_id$)
102        stmt$ += " ORDER BY person.person_id"
103        dbopenset stmt$
104        while dbrow()
105           print dbstring("person_id") + " " +
      dbstring("name") + " " + dbstring("phone") + " " +
      dbstring("type")
106        end while
107        dbcloseset
108     end subroutine
```

Exercises:

Word Search

```
y p z t c e l e s o x x d
e l i b a m l n a x x t b
t q x h o o e t g n e d i
a s t p s t l n e s t f n
e e a e a n i f n t t s t
r q t d s r o e b m a d r
c n p u t e p i n d b m e
i u e s c o s m t c l u s
d q b p b e u o l a e y n
b d u d o l x o l z l f i
r m o e o b s e p c w e m
o x h c r e d t b o b y r
w c g h t y j c r d s d m
```

column, create, dbclose, dbcloseset, dbexecute, dbfloat, dbint, dbopen, dbopenset, dbrow, dbstring, insert, query, relationship, row, select, sql, table, update

Problems

20.1. Take the "Big Program" from this chapter and modify it to create an application to keep track of a student's grades for several classes. You will need the following menu options to allow the user to:
- Enter a class code, assignment name, possible points, score on an assignment and store this information into a database table.
- Create a way for the student to see all of the grades for a single class after they enter the class code.
- Create an option to see a list of all classes with total points possible, total points scored, and percentage of scored vs. possible.

Chapter 21: Connecting with a Network

This chapter discusses how to use the BASIC-256 networking statements. Networking in BASIC-256 will allow for a simple "socket" connection using TCP (Transmission Control Protocol). This chapter is not meant to be a full introduction to TCP/IP socket programming.

Socket Connection:

TCP stream sockets create a connection between two computers or programs. Packets of information may be sent and received in a bi-directional (or two way) manner over the connection.

To start a connection we need one computer or program to act as a server (to wait for the incoming telephone call) and the other to be a client (to make the telephone call). Illustration 40 shows graphically how a stream connection is made.

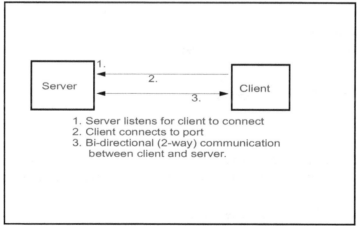

Illustration 40: Socket Communication

Just like with a telephone call, the person making the call (client) needs to know the phone number of the person they are calling (server). We call that number an IP address. BASIC-256 uses IP version 4 addresses that are usually expressed as four numbers separated by periods (A.B.C.D) where A, B, C, and D are integer values from 0 to 255.

In addition to having the IP address for the server, the client and server must also talk to each-other over a port. You can think of the port as a telephone extension in a large company. A person is assigned an extension (port) to answer (server) and if you want to talk to that person you (client) call that extension.

The port number may be between 0 and 65535 but various Internet and other applications have been reserved ports in the range of 0-1023. It is recommended that you avoid using these ports.

A Simple Server and Client:

```
1    # c21_simpleserver.kbs
2    # send a message to the client on port 999
3
4    print "listening to port 9999 on " + netaddress()
5    NetListen 9999
6    NetWrite "The simple server sent this message."
7    NetClose
```

Program 129: Simple Network Server

```
1    # c21_simpleclient.kbs
2    # connect to simple server and get the message
3    #
4    input "What is the address of the simple_server?",
     addr$
5    if addr$ = "" then addr$ = "127.0.0.1"
6    #
```

```
7      NetConnect addr$, 9999
8      print NetRead
9      NetClose
```

Program 130: Simple Network Client

```
listening to port 9999 on xx.xx.xx.xx
```

Sample Output 129: Simple Network Server

```
What is the address of the simple_server?
The simple server sent this message.
```

Sample Output 130: Simple Network Client

netaddress
netaddress ( )

Function that returns a string containing the numeric IPv4 network address for this machine.

New Concept

netlisten portnumber
netlisten (portnumbrer)
netlisten socketnumber, portnumber
netlisten (socketnumber, portnumber)

Open up a network connection (server) on a specific port address and wait for another program to connect. If *socketnumber* is not specified socket number zero (0) will be used.

New Concept

```
netclose
netclose ( )
netclose socketnumber
netclose ( socketnumber )
```

Close the specified network connection (socket). If *socketnumber* is not specified socket number zero (0) will be closed.

```
netwrite string
netwrite ( string )
netwrite socketnumber, string
netwrite ( socketnumber, string )
```

Send a string to the specified open network connection. If *socketnumber* is not specified socket number zero (0) will be written to.

```
netconnect servername, portnumber
netconnect ( servername, portnumber )
netconnect socketnumber, servername, portnumber
netconnect ( socketnumber, servername, portnumber
        )
```

Open a network connection (client) to a server. The IP address or host name of a server are specified in the *servername* argument, and the specific network port number. If *socketnumber* is not specified socket number zero (0) will be used for the connection.

	netread
	netread ( )
	netread (*socketnumber*)

New Concept

Read data from the specified network connection and return it as a string. This function is blocking (it will wait until data is received). If *socketnumber* is not specified socket number zero (0) will be read from.

Network Chat:

This example adds one new function (**netdata**) to the networking statements we have already introduced. Use of this new function will allow our network clients to process other events, like keystrokes, and then read network data only when there is data to be read.

The network chat program (Error: Reference source not found) combines the client and server program into one. If you start the application and it is unable to connect to a server the error is trapped and the program then becomes a server. This is one of many possible methods to allow a single program to fill both roles.

```
1    # c21_chat.kbs
2    # use port 9999 for simple chat
3
4    input "Chat to address (return for server or local
     host)?", addr$
5    if addr$ = "" then addr$ = "127.0.0.1"
6    #
7    # try to connect to server - if there is not one
     become one
8    try
9       NetConnect addr$, 9999
10   catch
```

```
11        print "starting server - waiting for chat client"
12        NetListen 9999
13   end try
14   print "connected"
15
16   while true
17      # get key pressed and send it
18      k = key
19      if k <> 0 then
20         call show(k)
21         netwrite string(k)
22      end if
23      # get key from network and show it
24      if NetData() then
25         k = int(NetRead())
26         call show(k)
27      end if
28      pause .01
29   end while
30   end
31
32   subroutine show(keyvalue)
33      if keyvalue=16777220 then
34         print
35      else
36         print chr(keyvalue);
37      end if
38   end subroutine
```

Program 131: Network Chat

The following is observed when the user on the client types the message "HI SERVER" and then the user on the server types "HI CLIENT".

```
Chat to address (return for server or local
host)?
starting server - waiting for chat client
```

```
          connected
          HI SERVER
          HI CLIENT
```

Sample Output 131.1: Network Chat (Server)


```
          Chat to address (return for server or local
          host)?
          connected
          HI SERVER
          HI CLIENT
```

Sample Output 131.2: Network Chat (Client)

New Concept

`netdata` or `netdata()`
`netdata ( socketnumbr )`

Returns true if there is network data waiting to be read. This allows for the program to continue operations without waiting for a network packet to arrive.

Big Program

The big program this chapter creates a two player networked tank battle game. Each player is the white tank on their screen and the other player is the black tank. Use the arrow keys to rotate and move. Shoot with the space bar.


```
1       # c21_battle.kbs
```

```
2      # uses port 9998 for server
3
4      spritedim 4
5      call tanksprite(0,white) # me
6      call tanksprite(1,black) # opponent
7      call projectilesprite(2,blue) # my shot
8      call projectilesprite(3,red) # opponent shot
9
10     kspace = 32
11     kleft = 16777234
12     kright = 16777236
13     kup = 16777235
14     kdown = 16777237
15
16     dr = pi / 20   # direction change
17     dxy = 2.5 # move speed
18     shotdxy = 5    # shot move speed
19     port = 9998    # port to communicate on
20
21     print "Tank Battle - You are the white tank."
22     print "Your mission is to shoot and kill the"
23     print "black one. Use arrows to move and"
24     print "space to shoot."
25     print
26
27     input "Are you the server? (y or n)", mode$
28     if mode$ = "y" then
29        print "You are the server.  Waiting for a client
       to connect."
30        NetListen port
31     else
32        input "Server Address to connect to (return for
       local host)?", addr$
33        if addr$ = "" then addr$ = "127.0.0.1"
34        NetConnect addr$, port
35     end if
36
37     # set my default position and send to my opponent
38     x = 100
```

```
39      y = 100
40      r = 0
41      # projectile position direction and visible
42      p = false
43      px = 0
44      py = 0
45      pr = 0
46      call writeposition(x,y,r,p,px,py,pr)
47
48
49      # update the screen
50      color green
51      rect 0, 0, graphwidth, graphheight
52      spriteshow 0
53      spriteshow 1
54      spriteplace 0, x, y, 1, r
55      while true
56          # get key pressed and move tank on the screen
57          k = key
58          if k <> 0 then
59              if k = kup then
60                  x = ( graphwidth + x + sin(r) * dxy ) %
        graphwidth
61                  y = ( graphheight + y - cos(r) * dxy ) %
        graphheight
62              end if
63              if k = kdown then
64                  x = ( graphwidth + x - sin(r) * dxy ) %
        graphwidth
65                  y = ( graphheight + y + cos(r) * dxy ) %
        graphheight
66              end if
67              if k = kleft then r = r - dr
68              if k = kright then r = r + dr
69              if k = kspace then
70                  pr = r
71                  px = x
72                  py = y
73                  p = true
```

```
74                    spriteshow 2
75                end if
76                spriteplace 0, x, y, 1, r
77                call writeposition( x, y, r, p, px, py, pr )
78                if spritecollide( 0, 1 ) then
79                    netwrite "F"
80                    print "You just ran into the other tank and
        you both died. Game Over."
81                    end
82                end if
83            end if
84        # move my projectile (if there is one)
85        if p then
86            px = px + sin( pr ) * shotdxy
87            py = py - cos( pr ) * shotdxy
88            spriteplace 2, px, py, 1, pr
89            if spritecollide( 1, 2 ) then
90                NetWrite "W"
91                print "You killed your opponent. Game over."
92                end
93            end if
94            if px < 0 or px > graphwidth or py < 0 or py >
        graphheight then
95                p = false
96                spritehide 2
97            end if
98            call writeposition( x, y, r, p, px, py, pr )
99        end if
100       #
101       # get position from network and
102       # set location variables for the opponent
103       # flip the coordinates as we decode
104       while NetData()
105           position$ = NetRead()
106           while position$ <> ""
107               if left(position$,1) = "W" then
108                   print "You Died. - Game Over"
109                   end
110               end if
```

```
111                    if left(position$,1) = "F" then
112                        print "You were hit and you both died. -
       Game Over"
113                        end
114                    end if
115                    op_x = graphwidth - unpad( ref( position$ ),
       3)
116                    op_y = graphheight -
       unpad( ref( position$ ), 3)
117                    op_r = pi + unpad( ref( position$ ), 5)
118                    op_p = unpad( ref( position$ ), 1)
119                    op_px = graphwidth -
       unpad( ref( position$ ), 3)
120                    op_py = graphheight -
       unpad( ref( position$ ), 3)
121                    op_pr = pi + unpad( ref( position$ ), 5)
122                    # display opponent
123                    spriteplace 1, op_x, op_y, 1, op_r
124                    if op_p then
125                        spriteshow 3
126                        spriteplace 3, op_px, op_py, 1, op_pr
127                    else
128                        spritehide 3
129                    end if
130                end while
131            end while
132            #
133            pause .05
134        end while
135
136    subroutine writeposition(x,y,r,p,px,py,pr)
137        position$ =  lpad$( int( x ), 3 ) + lpad$
       ( int( y ), 3 ) + lpad$( r, 5 ) + lpad$( p, 1 ) +
       lpad$( int( px ), 3 ) + lpad$( int( py ), 3 ) + lpad$
       ( pr, 5 )
138        NetWrite position$
139    end subroutine
140
141    function lpad$( n, l )
```

```
142        # return a number left padded in spaces
143        s$ = left( n, l )
144        while length( s$ ) < l
145           s$ = " " + s$
146        end while
147        return s$
148    end function
149
150    function unpad( ref( l$ ), l )
151        # return a number at the begining padded in l
       spaces
152        # and shorten the string by l that we just pulled
       off
153        n = float( left( l$, l ) )
154        if length( l$ ) > l then
155           l$ = mid( l$, l + 1, 99999 )
156        else
157           l$ = ""
158        end if
159        return n
160    end function
161
162    subroutine tanksprite( spritenumber , c )
163        color c
164        spritepoly spritenumber, {0,0, 7,0, 7,7, 14,7,
       20,0, 26,7, 33,7, 33,0, 40,0, 40,40, 33,40, 33,33,
       7,33, 7,40, 0,40}
165    end subroutine
166
167    subroutine projectilesprite( spritenumber, c)
168        color c
169        spritepoly spritenumber, {3,0, 3,8, 0,8}
170    end subroutine
```

Program 132: Network Tank Battle

Sample Output 43: Adding Machine - Using Exit While

Exercises:

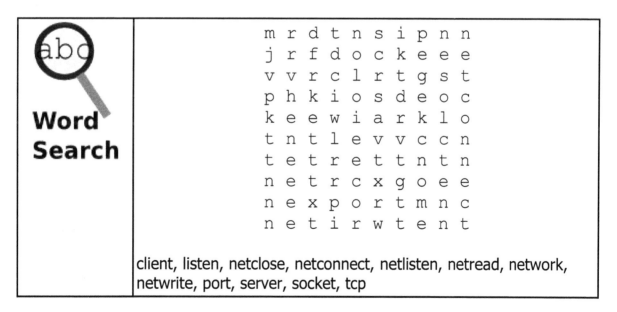

Word Search	m r d t n s i p n n j r f d o c k e e e v v r c l r t g s t p h k i o s d e o c k e e w i a r k l o t n t l e v v c c n t e t r e t t n t n n e t r c x g o e e n e x p o r t m n c n e t i r w t e n t

client, listen, netclose, netconnect, netlisten, netread, network, netwrite, port, server, socket, tcp

Problems

21.1. Modify Problem 12.4 to create a network client/server 2 player "ping-pong" game.

21.2. Write a simple server/client rock-paper-scissors game where two players will compete.

21.3. Write a complex network chat server that can connect to several clients at once. You will need a server process to assign each client a different port on the server for the actual chat traffic.

Appendix A: Loading BASIC-256 on your Windows PC

This chapter will walk you step by step through downloading and installing BASIC-256 on your Microsoft Windows PC. The instructions are written for Windows XP with Firefox as your Web browser. Your specific configuration and installation may be different but the general steps should be similar.

1 – Download:

Connect to the Internet and navigate to the Web site http://www.basic256.org and follow the download link. Once you are at the Sourceforge project page click on the green "Download Now!"button (Illustration 41) to start the download process.

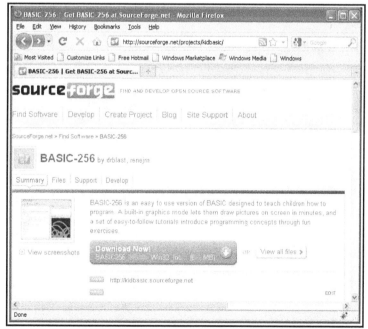

Illustration 41: BASIC-256 on Sourceforge

The download process may ask you what you want to do with the file. Click the "Save File" button (Illustration 42).

Illustration 42: Saving Install File

Firefox should display the "Downloads" window and actually download the BASIC-256 installer. When it is finished it should look like Illustration 43. Do not close this window quite yet, you will need it to start the Installation.

Illustration 43: File Downloaded

2 – Installing:

Once the file has finished downloading (Illustration 43) use your mouse and click on the file from the download list. You will then see one or two dialogs asking if you really want to execute this file (Illustration 44) (Illustration 45). You need to click the "OK" or "Run" buttons on these dialogs.

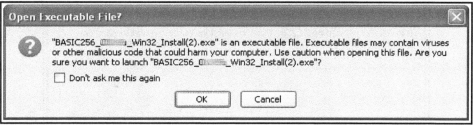

Illustration 44: Open File Warning

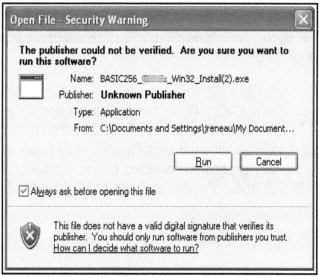

Illustration 45: Open File Security Warning

After the security warnings are cleared you will see the actual BASIC-256 Installer application. Click the "Next>" button on the first screen (Illustration 46).

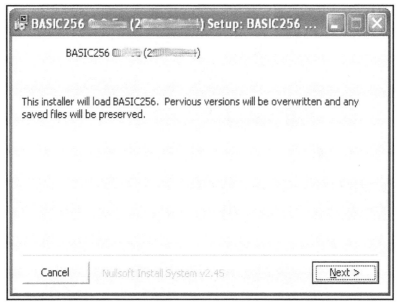

Illustration 46: Installer - Welcome Screen

Read and agree to the GNU GPL software license and click on "I Agree" (Illustration 47). The GNU GPL license is one of the most commonly used "Open Source" and"Free" license to software. You have the right to use, give away, and modify the programs released under the GPL. This license only relates to the BASIC-256 software and not the contents of this book.

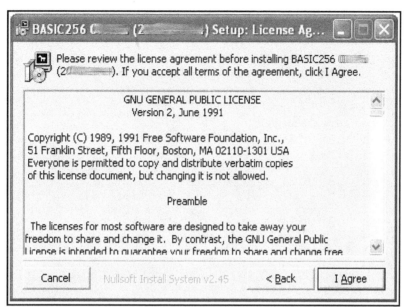

Illustration 47: Installer - GPL License Screen

The next Installer screen asks you what you want to install (Illustration 48). If you are installing BASIC-256 to a USB or other type of removable drive then it is suggested that you un-check the "Start Menu Shortcuts". For most users who are installing to a hard drive, should do a complete install. Click "Next>".

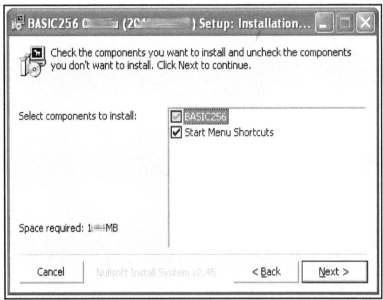

Illustration 48: Installer - What to Install

Illustration 49 shows the last screen before the install begins. This screen asks you what folder to install the BASIC-256 executable files into. If you are installing to your hard drive then you should accept the default path.

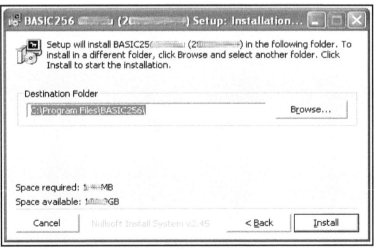

Illustration 49: Installer - Where to Install

The installation is complete when you see this screen (Illustration 50). Click "Close".

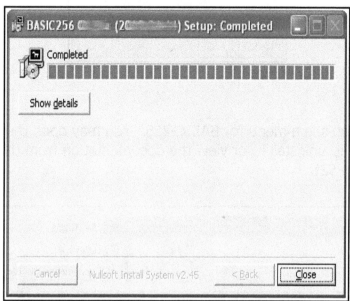

Illustration 50: Installer - Complete

3 – Starting BASIC-256

The installation is complete. You may now click on the Windows "Start" button and then "All Programs >" (Illustration 51).

Illustration 51: XP Start Button

You will then see a menu for BASIC-256. You may open the program by clicking on it, uninstall it, or view the documentation from this menu (Illustration 52).

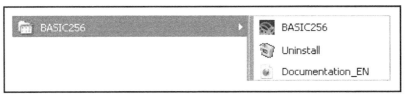

Illustration 52: BASIC-256 Menu from All Programs

Appendix B: Color Names and Numbers

Listing of standard color names used in the *color* statement. The corresponding RGB values are also listed.

Color	RGB Values	Swatch
black	0, 0, 0	
white	255, 255, 255	
red	255, 0, 0	
darkred	128, 0, 0	
green	0, 255, 0	
darkgreen	0, 128, 0	
blue	0, 0, 255	
darkblue	0, 0, 128	
cyan	0, 255, 255	
darkcyan	0, 128, 128	
purple	255, 0, 255	
darkpurple	128, 0, 128	
yellow	255, 255, 0	
darkyellow	128, 128, 0	
orange	255, 102, 0	
darkorange	176, 61, 0	
gray /grey	160, 160, 160	
darkgray / darkgrey	128, 128, 128	
clear		

Appendix C: Musical Tones

This chart will help you in converting the keys on a piano into frequencies to use in the **sound** statement.

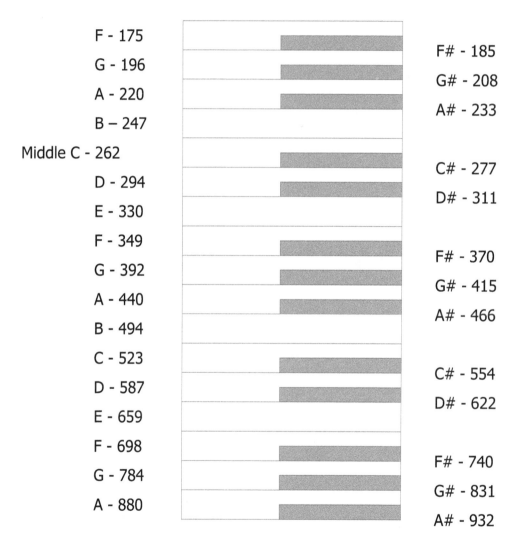

F - 175

F# - 185

G - 196

G# - 208

A - 220

A# - 233

B – 247

Middle C - 262

C# - 277

D - 294

D# - 311

E - 330

F - 349

F# - 370

G - 392

G# - 415

A - 440

A# - 466

B - 494

C - 523

C# - 554

D - 587

D# - 622

E - 659

F - 698

F# - 740

G - 784

G# - 831

A - 880

A# - 932

Appendix D: Key Values

Key values are returned by the *key()* function and represent the last keyboard key pressed since the key was last read. This table lists the commonly used key values for the standard English keyboard. Other key values exist.

English (EN) Keyboard Codes										
Key	**#**		**Key**	**#**		**Key**	**#**		**Key**	**#**
Space	32		A	65		L	76		W	87
0	48		B	66		M	77		X	88
1	49		C	67		N	78		Y	89
2	50		D	68		O	79		Z	90
3	51		E	69		P	80		ESC	16777216
4	52		F	70		Q	81		Backspace	16777219
5	53		G	71		R	82		Enter	16777220
6	54		H	72		S	83		Left Arrow	16777234
7	55		I	73		T	84		Up Arrow	16777235
8	56		J	74		U	85		Right Arrow	16777236
9	57		K	75		V	86		Down Arrow	16777237

Appendix E: Unicode Character Values – Latin (English)

This table shows the Unicode character values for standard Latin (English) letters and symbols. These values correspond with the ASCII values that have been used since the 1960's. Additional character sets are available at http://www.unicode.org.

CHR	#	CHR	#	CHR	#	CHR	#	CHR	#	CHR	#
NUL	0	SYN	22	,	44	B	66	X	88	n	110
SOH	1	ETB	23	-	45	C	67	Y	89	o	111
STX	2	CAN	24	.	46	D	68	Z	90	p	112
ETX	3	EM	25	/	47	E	69	[	91	q	113
ET	4	SUB	26	0	48	F	70	\	92	r	114
ENQ	5	ESC	27	1	49	G	71	]	93	s	115
ACK	6	FS	28	2	50	H	72	^	94	t	116
BEL	7	GS	28	3	51	I	73	_	95	u	117
BS	8	RS	30	4	52	J	74	`	96	v	118
HT	9	US	31	5	53	K	75	a	97	w	119
LF	10	Space	32	6	54	L	76	b	98	x	120
VT	11	!	33	7	55	M	77	c	99	y	121
FF	12	"	34	8	56	N	78	d	100	z	122
CR	13	#	35	9	57	O	79	e	101	{	123
SO	14	$	36	:	58	P	80	f	102			124
SI	15	%	37	;	59	Q	81	g	103	}	125
DLE	16	&	38	<	60	R	82	h	104	~	126
DC1	17	'	39	=	61	S	83	i	105	DEL	127
DC2	18	(	40	>	62	T	84	j	106		
DC3	19	)	41	?	63	U	85	k	107		
DC4	20	*	42	@	64	V	86	l	108		
NAK	21	+	43	A	65	W	87	m	109		

0-31 and 127 are non-printable.
Adapted from the Unicode Standard 5.2

Appendix F: Reserved Words

These are the words that the BASIC-256 language uses to perform various tasks. You may not use any of these words for variable names or labels for the GOTO and GOSUB statements

```
#                           cyan
abs                         dark
acos                        darkblue
and                         darkcyan
arc                         darkgeeen
asc                         darkgray
asin                        darkgrey
atan                        darkorange
black                       darkpurple
blue                        darkred
call                        darkyellow
catch                       day
ceil                        dbclose
changedir                   dbcloseset
chord                       dbexecute
chr                         dbfloat
circle                      dbint
clear                       dbnull
clg                         dbopen
clickb                      dbopenset
clickclear                  dbrow
clickx                      dbstring
clicky                      debuginfo
close                       degrees
cls                         dim
color                       dir
colour                      do
confirm                     editvisible
continue                    else
continuedo                  end
continuefor                 endfunction
continuewhile               endif
cos                         endsubroutine
count                       endtry
countx                      endwhile
currentdir                  eof
```

```
error_arrayindex                    error_none
error_arrayindexmissing             error_nonnumeric
error_arraysizelarge                error_nosuchvariable
error_arraysizesmall                error_notanumber
error_byref                         error_notimplemented
error_byreftype                     error_penwidth
error_colornumber                   error_permission
error_dbcolno                       error_polyarray
error_dbconnnumber                  error_polypoints
error_dbnotopen                     error_printernotoff
error_dbnotset                      error_printernoton
error_dbnotsetrow                   error_printeropen
error_dbopen                        error_putbitformat
error_dbquery                       error_radix
error_dbsetnumber                   error_radixstring
error_divzero                       error_rgb
error_filenotopen                   error_spritena
error_filenumber                    error_spritenumber
error_fileopen                      error_spriteslice
error_filereset                     error_strend
error_filewrite                     error_stringmaxlen
error_folder                        error_strneglen
error_fontsize                      error_strstart
error_fontweight                    exists
error_for1                          exitdo
error_for2                          exitfor
error_freedb                        exitwhile
error_freedbset                     exp
error_freefile                      explode
error_freenet                       explodex
error_imagefile                     false
error_imagesavetype                 fastgraphics
error_imagescale                    float
error_infinity                      floor
error_lograngе                      font
error_netaccept                     for
error_netbind                       freedb
error_netconn                       freedbset
error_nethost                       freefile
error_netnone                       freenet
error_netread                       frombinary
error_netsock                       fromhex
error_netsocknumber                 fromoctal
error_netsockopt                    fromradix
error_netwrite                      getbrushcolor
```

getcolor
getpenwidth
getsetting
getslice
global
gosub
goto
graphheight
graphsize
graphwidth
gray
green
grey
hour
if
imgload
imgsave
implode
include
input
instr
instrx
int
key
kill
lasterror
lasterrorextra
lasterrorline
lasterrormessage
left
length
line
log
log10
lower
md5
mid
minute
month
mouseb
mousex
mousey
msec
netaddress
netclose

netconnect
netdata
netlisten
netread
netwritenext
next
not
offerror
onerror
open
openb
or
orange
ostype
outputvisible
pause
penwidth
pi
pie
pixel
plot
poly
portin
portout
print
printercancel
printeroff
printeron
printerpage
purple
putslice
radians
rand
read
readbyte
readline
rect
red
redim
ref
refresh
rem
replace
replacex
reset

return	tan
rgb	text
right	textheight
say	textwidth
second	then
seek	throwerror
setsetting	to
sin	tobinary
size	tohex
sound	tooctal
spritecollide	toradix
spritedim	true
spriteh	try
spritehide	until
spriteload	upper
spritemove	version
spriteplace	volume
spritepoly	wavplay
spriteshow	wavstop
spriteslice	wavwait
spritev	while
spritew	white
spritex	write
spritey	writebyte
sqr	writeline
stamp	xor
step	year
string	yellow
system	

Appendix G: Errors and Warnings

Error #		Error Description (EN)
0	ERROR_NONE	
2	ERROR_FOR1	"Illegal FOR – start number > end number"
3	ERROR_FOR2	"Illegal FOR – start number < end number"
5	ERROR_FILENUMBER	"Invalid File Number"
6	ERROR_FILEOPEN	"Unable to open file"
7	ERROR_FILENOTOPEN	"File not open."
8	ERROR_FILEWRITE	"Unable to write to file"
9	ERROR_FILERESET	"Unable to reset file"
10	ERROR_ARRAYSIZELARGE	"Array dimension too large"
11	ERROR_ARRAYSIZESMALL	"Array dimension too small"
12	ERROR_NOSUCHVARIABLE	"Unknown variable"
15	ERROR_ARRAYINDEX	"Array index out of bounds"
16	ERROR_STRNEGLEN	"Substring length less that zero"
17	ERROR_STRSTART	"Starting position less than zero"
18	ERROR_STREND	"String not long enough for given starting character"
19	ERROR_NONNUMERIC	"Non-numeric value in numeric expression"
20	ERROR_RGB	"RGB Color values must be in the range of 0 to 255."
21	ERROR_PUTBITFORMAT	"String input to putbit incorrect."
22	ERROR_POLYARRAY	"Argument not an array for poly()/stamp()"
23	ERROR_POLYPOINTS	"Not enough points in array for poly()/stamp()"
24	ERROR_IMAGEFILE	"Unable to load image file."
25	ERROR_SPRITENUMBER	"Sprite number out of range."
26	ERROR_SPRITENA	"Sprite has not been assigned."
27	ERROR_SPRITESLICE	"Unable to slice image."
28	ERROR_FOLDER	"Invalid directory name."

29	ERROR_INFINITY	"Operation returned infinity."
30	ERROR_DBOPEN	"Unable to open SQLITE database."
31	ERROR_DBQUERY	"Database query error (message follows)."
32	ERROR_DBNOTOPEN	"Database must be opened first."
33	ERROR_DBCOLNO	"Column number out of range."
34	ERROR_DBNOTSET	"Record set must be opened first."
35	ERROR_TYPECONV	"Unable to convert string to number."
36	ERROR_NETSOCK	"Error opening network socket."
37	ERROR_NETHOST	"Error finding network host."
38	ERROR_NETCONN	"Unable to connect to network host."
39	ERROR_NETREAD	"Unable to read from network connection."
40	ERROR_NETNONE	"Network connection has not been opened."
41	ERROR_NETWRITE	"Unable to write to network connection."
42	ERROR_NETSOCKOPT	"Unable to set network socket options."
43	ERROR_NETBIND	"Unable to bind network socket."
44	ERROR_NETACCEPT	"Unable to accept network connection."
45	ERROR_NETSOCKNUMBER	"Invalid Socket Number"
46	ERROR_PERMISSION	"You do not have permission to use this statement/function."
47	ERROR_IMAGESAVETYPE	"Invalid image save type."
50	ERROR_DIVZERO	"Division by zero"
51	ERROR_BYREF	"Function/Subroutine expecting variable reference in call"
52	ERROR_BYREFTYPE	"Function/Subroutine variable incorrect reference type in call"
53	ERROR_FREEFILE	"There are no free file numbers to allocate"
54	ERROR_FREENET	"There are no free network connections to allocate"
55	ERROR_FREEDB	"There are no free database connections to allocate"
56	ERROR_DBCONNNUMBER	"Invalid Database Connection Number"
57	ERROR_FREEDBSET	"There are no free data sets to allocate for that

		database connection"
58	ERROR_DBSETNUMBER	"Invalid data set number"
59	ERROR_DBNOTSETROW	"You must advance the data set using DBROW before you can read data from it"
60	ERROR_PENWIDTH	"Drawing pen width must be a non-negative number"
61	ERROR_COLORNUMBER	"Color values must be in the range of -1 to 16,777,215"
62	ERROR_ARRAYINDEXMISSING	"Array variable %VARNAME% has no value without an index"
63	ERROR_IMAGESCALE	"Image scale must be greater than or equal to zero"
64	ERROR_FONTSIZE	"Font size, in points, must be greater than or equal to zero"
65	ERROR_FONTWEIGHT	"Font weight must be greater than or equal to zero"
66	ERROR_RADIXSTRING	"Unable to convert radix string back to a decimal number"
67	ERROR_RADIX	"Radix conversion base muse be between 2 and 36"
68	ERROR_LOGRANGE	"Unable to calculate the logarithm or root of a negative number"
69	ERROR_STRINGMAXLEN	"String exceeds maximum length of 16,777,216 characters"
70	ERROR_NOTANUMBER	"Mathematical operation returned an undefined value"
71	ERROR_PRINTERNOTON	"Printer is not on."
72	ERROR_PRINTERNOTOFF	"Printing is already on."
73	ERROR_PRINTEROPEN	"Unable to open printer."
65535	ERROR_NOTIMPLEMENTED	"Feature not implemented in this environment."

WARNING #		Error Description (EN)
65537	WARNING_TYPECONV	"Unable to convert string to number, zero used"

Appendix H: Glossary

Glossary of terms used in this book.

algorithm – A step-by-step process for solving a problem.

angle – An angle is formed when two line segments (or rays) start at the same point on a plane. An angle's measurement is the amount of rotation from one ray to another on the plane and is typically expressed in radians or degrees.

argument – A data value included in a statement or function call used to pass information. In BASIC-256 argument values are not changed by the statement or function.

array – A collection of data, stored in the computer's memory, that is accessed by using one or more integer indexes. See also numeric array, one dimensional array, string array, and two dimensional array.

ASCII – (acronym for American Standard Code for Information Interchange) Defines a numeric code used to represent letters and symbols used in the English Language. See also Unicode.

asynchronous – Process or statements happening at one after the other.

Boolean Algebra – The algebra of true/false values created by Charles Boole over 150 years ago.

Cartesian Coordinate System – Uniquely identify a point on a plane by a pair of distances from the origin (0,0). The two distances are measured on perpendicular axes.

column (database) – defines a single piece of information that will be common to all rows of a database table.

constant – A value that can not be changed.

data structure – is a way to store and use information efficiently in a computer system

database – An organized collection of data. Most databases are computerized and consist of tables of similar information that are broken into rows and columns. See also: column, row, SQL, and table.

degrees – A unit of angular measure. Angles on a plane can have measures in degrees of 0 to 360. A right angle is 90 degrees. See also angle and radians.

empty string – A string with no characters and a length of zero (0). Represented by two quotation marks (""). See also string.

false – Boolean value representing not true. In BASIC-256 it is actually short hand for the integer zero (0). See also Boolean Algebra and true.

floating point number – A numeric value that may or may not contain a decimal point. Typically floating point numbers have a range of $\pm 1.7 \times 10^{\pm 308}$ with 15 digits of precision.

font – A style of drawing letters.

frequency – The number of occurrences of an event over a specific period of time. See also hertz.

function – A special type of statement in BASIC-256 that may take zero or more values, make calculations, and return information to your program.

graphics output area – The area on the screen where drawing is displayed.

hertz (hz) – Measure of frequency in cycles per second. Named for German physicist Heinrich Hertz. See also frequency.

integer – A numeric value with no decimal point. A whole number. Typically has a range of –2,147,483,648 to 2,147,483,647.

IP address – Short for Internet Protocol address. An IP address is a numeric label assigned to a device on a network.

label – A name associated with a specific place in the program. Used for jumping to with the **goto** and **gosub** statements.

list – A collection of values that can be used to assign arrays and in some statements. In BASIC-256 lists are represented as comma (,) separated values inside a set of curly-braces ({}).

logical error – An error that causes the program to not perform as expected.

named constant – A value that is represented by a name but can not be changed.

numeric array – An array of numbers.

numeric variable – A variable that can be used to store integer or floating point numbers.

one dimensional array - A structure in memory that holds a list of data that is addressed by a single index. See also array.

operator – Acts upon one or two pieces of data to perform an action.

pixel – Smallest addressable point on a computer display screen.

point – Measurement of text – 1 point = 1/72". A character set in 12 point will be 12/72" or 1/6" tall.

port – A software endpoint number used to create and communicate on a socket.

pseudocode – Description of what a program needs to do in a natural (non-computer) language. This word contains the prefix "pseudo" which means false and "code" for programming text.

radian - A unit of angular measure. Angles on a plane can have measures in radians of 0 to 2π. A right angle is π/2 degrees. See also angle and degrees.

radius – Distance from a circle to it's center. Also, ½ of a circle's diameter.

RGB – Acronym for Red Green Blue. Light is made up of these three colors.

row (database) – Also called a record or tuple. A row can be thought of as a single member of a table.

socket – A software endpoint that allows for bi-directional (2 way) network communications between two process on a single computer or two computers.

sprite – An image that is integrated into a graphical scene.

SQL – Acronym for Structured Query Language. SQL is the most widely used language to manipulate data in a relational database.

statement – A single complete action. Statements perform something and do not return a value.

string – A sequence of characters (letters, numbers, and symbols). String constants are surrounded by double quotation marks (").

string array – An array of strings.

string variable – A variable that can be used to store string values. A string variable is denoted by placing a dollar sign ($) after the variable name.

sub-string – Part of a larger string.

subroutine – A block of code or portion of a larger program that performs a task independently from the rest of the program. A piece that can be used and re-used by many parts of a program.

syntax error – An error with the structure of a statement so that the program will not execute.

synchronous – Happening at the same time.

table (database) – Data organized into rows and columns. A table has a specific number of defined columns and zero or more rows.

transparent – Able to see through.

text output area – The area of the screen where plain text and errors is displayed.

true – Boolean value representing not false. In BASIC-256 it is actually short hand for the integer one (1). See also Boolean Algebra and false.

two dimensional array – A structure in memory that will hold rows and columns of data. See also array.

Unicode – The modern standard used to represent characters and symbols of all of the world's languages as integer numbers.

variable – A named storage location in the computer's memory that can be changed or varied.

www.ingramcontent.com/pod-product-compliance
Lightning Source LLC
Chambersburg PA
CBHW080148060326
40689CB00018B/3895